A Beam of Divine Glory

or

The Unchangeableness of God Opened, Vindicated, and Improved

whereunto is added

The Soul's Rest in God

by Edward Pearse
Pastor of St. Margaret's Westminster

Edited by Rev. Don Kistler

Soli Deo Gloria Publications
. . . for instruction in righteousness . . .

Soli Deo Gloria Publications
P.O. Box 451, Morgan, PA 15064
(412) 221-1901/FAX 221-1902

*

A Beam of Divine Glory was first published in 1674 in London. This Soli Deo Gloria reprint, in which spelling, grammatical, and formatting changes have been made, is © 1998 by Don Kistler and Soli Deo Gloria. All rights reserved. Printed in the USA.

*

ISBN 1-57358-067-8

Contents

A Beam of Divine Glory

The Soul's Rest in God

To the Reader

The unchangeableness of God is one of those perfections of His whereby He is, in a peculiar manner, distinguished from the creatures. The creatures are made up of changes. Their beings, life, and conditions are subject to many changes. But God knows none of these changes. His being is most immutable. His life is the most even, constant, uniform, serene life. His happiness is at all times alike and the same. "God does always abide in the same likeness," said one of the ancients. "With Him there is no variableness nor shadow of change."

Now there is an instinct in us whereby we are moved to desire unchangeableness. Everything naturally desires its perfection; man, therefore, being a reasonable creature, and finding himself subject to many changes, longs after a perfect state, which is to be unchangeable. He would fain come to an unchangeable life, to an unchangeable happiness. Now what we cannot find or attain unto ourselves, we should aspire after by attaining union and conjunction with our Maker. Everything is made perfect by reaching or attaining its first cause or principle. God is the fountain of life, the fountain of unchangeableness, so far as unchangeableness is communicable to the creatures. Indeed, in a strict and proper sense, unchangeableness is one of the incommunicable attributes of God; none but God is simply and absolutely unchangeable, or can be so. It implies a contradiction to suppose a creature intrinsically and in its own nature, not to be under a possibility of change; but yet, after a sort, the creatures may be made unchangeable in having an unchangeable life, an unchangeable happiness given to them by some kind of participation with God, who is the chief good, and who has all life and happiness in Himself. Thus the holy angels, who are not simply and absolutely unchangeable in themselves, yet enjoy an unchangeable life and happiness, by way of sharing in the sight of God and communion with God. We should therefore aspire after the sight of God, and press after the most perfect adherence to Him. God only is the center of unchangeableness, and by fixing our hearts in Him we shall, after a time, become unchangeable. "Join your heart to eternity," said Augustine, "and you yourself shall be eternal."

The author of the following discourse now has a blessed experience of what that shared unchangeableness is (if we may so call it) which glorified souls have in the divine presence by having communion with God, the first unchangeable being. While he lived here on earth, he saw many changes passing over himself, both as to his person and condition. This put him upon the contemplation of the unchangeableness of God, and caused him to seek for that rest in God which he could not find in himself, nor in anything here below. Those who observed his spirit clearly perceived that he was much quickened and helped, as to his spiritual state, by meditating much on a holy rest in God. So it is not to be doubted that, if we take the same course and keep the eye of our minds fixed on God, laboring to take all our rest and satisfaction in Him, there shall we find that true quiet for our souls which we vainly seek after in the variety of objects here below. And the serious perusing of these discourses, which carry much of the impress of the author's spirit upon them, may be of good use to us, to help us attain such an end.

The author had no thoughts at first of bringing forth these sermons unto public view, but, being much persuaded hereunto by his nearest relation, at last he yielded to that importunity and perfected them with his own hand. The rest of his notes being left in characters, it is much to be feared these are the last sermons of his that are likely to see the light.

To close, I may only add that it is matter of sad lamentation to us to consider how many of the faithful servants of God who have been eminent in their generations have been taken away in a few years. Certainly it becomes us to bewail greatly the deaths of so many godly ministers, and, since the harvest is great and the faithful laborers are but few, we should pray the Lord of the harvest that He would thrust forth laborers into the vineyard.

Thine in the Lord Christ,

John Howe

Chapter One

Wherein way is made to the text; the words thereof opened; the foundation of our intended discourse laid, and the principal matters to be considered in the prosecution of it hinted at

It is a great, as well as true, observation which I have read in a learned man: namely that all the many various attributes of God mentioned in the Scripture are no other than His very essence, and are ascribed to Him to help us in our conceptions and understandings of Him, who are not able to apprehend what may be known of God under any one name or notion or by any one act of the intellect. We read (you know) of His power, His wisdom, His holiness, His justice, His goodness, His faithfulness, His all-sufficiency, and the like, all which are not distinguished in Him, either from Himself or from one another, but are all one and the same God revealed and manifested to us under various notions, and that to help us better to conceive and apprehend Him, and also to perform our homage and worship of Him. Accordingly we may say, "The holiness of God is God; the wisdom of God is God; the power of God is God; the goodness of God is God." And, to come to my text, the unchangeableness of God is God; and indeed the unchangeableness of God is God manifested and revealed under a sweet and blessed, as well as a glorious, notion to us, under such a notion as conduces much to the quickening and encouraging of our faith and love, our comfort and obedience, in Him and to Him. And so indeed the text represents it: "I am the Lord, I change not; therefore ye sons of Jacob are not consumed" (Malachi 3:6). In these words we have two things to be noted:

1. Here is a display or representation of God in one ray or beam of His divine glory, and that is His unchangeableness: "I am the Lord, I change not," or, "I the Lord am not changed." For it may be read either actively or passively and the sense will be the same. "I change not. I am not altered or varied at all. What I was I am; what I am I still shall be." God here (as a judicious expositor observed) tactically opposes Himself to mortal men, and removes and renounces all wavering and inconstancy from Himself. "I change not." It is as if He should have said, "Men die, but I live; men change, but I change not. I am still the same."

2. Here is a mention or declaration of the blessed fruit or issue of this glorious perfection of God in reference to His church and people, and that is their preservation from destruction: "Therefore ye sons of Jacob are not consumed."

Here two things must be inquired into: first, who are we to understand by "the sons of Jacob?" And second, what are we to understand by their being not consumed?

Who are we to understand by "the sons of Jacob?" By "the sons of Jacob" here we are to understand God's professing church and people. We read in

Scripture of the house of Jacob, the seed of Jacob, and the sons of Jacob, by all which are meant God's church and people whom He takes into covenant with Himself and makes the objects of His love. And this will be evident by comparing my text with Malachi 1:2 where God says expressly that "I have loved you," and again, "I loved Jacob." What are we to understand by their being not consumed? It imports and carries in it these two things: an exemption from temporal ruin and a preservation from eternal destruction.

An exemption from temporal ruin. "Therefore ye are not consumed," that is, "Therefore you are not cut off from being a people; therefore you are not utterly broken by My judgments. It is true, some afflictions you have had, yes, great afflictions, but still you live, still you are a people; you are preserved from utter ruin and destruction. And why so? Not because you have not deserved to be utterly cut off and destroyed, but because I am unchangeable. I am the Lord, I change not; therefore ye sons of Jacob are not consumed."

A preservation from eternal destruction. "Therefore ye are not consumed," that is, "Therefore you are not in hell; therefore you are not under the eternal revelations of My wrath, which (alas!) is what you have deserved." It is as if God should say to them, "True, you have had affliction, but (alas!) it has been nothing to what your sins deserve. Your sins have been many and great against Me, such as deserved utter ruin, yes, eternal destruction, an utter consumption both of body and soul forever, and this would have been your portion long ago were you not dealing

with an unchangeable God. It is not your desert, but
My unchangeableness which is the sole cause why
you are not utterly and eternally destroyed."

In short, the design of the whole was to upbraid
them with their sins, and particularly their ingrati-
tude, and withal to let them know that the reason
why it was no worse with them than it was, yes, why
they were not totally and eternally destroyed, was not
because they did not deserve to have had it so, but
because their God was unchangeable. In saying, "I
am the Lord, I change not," God seems to be saying
to them: "You complain of Me, and have hard
thoughts of Me, because it is with you as it is and I
do not presently arise for your help. But let Me tell
you, it is well for you that it is not ten thousand
times worse with you than it is. It is well you are a
people; it is well you are not among the damned.
Sure I am, you highly deserved to have had it so with
you; you are a sinful, sinning, rebellious people, a
people that has deserved to be destroyed ten thousand times over. I have done great things for you
above any people. I have shown you much love, but
you have not walked suitably and answerably to the
great things I have done for you, nor the great love I
have shown to you. No, you have abused all, and
sinned against Me after all, and that with a high
hand whereby you have deserved to be utterly consumed and destroyed. And, indeed, had I not been
an unchangeable God, consumed and destroyed you
would have been long ago. I see that in you and
among you for which I might justly destroy you, and
that forever; and nothing but my own unchangeableness keeps you alive. Should you therefore com-

plain of Me? Should you not rather admire My patience and forbearance so long with you and towards you? Truly it is a miracle of grace, goodness,
and patience in Me that you have not been long
since destroyed once for all."

This I take to be the true scope and meaning of
the Word, the sum of which, together with the
foundation of my intended discourse from them, I
shall give you in this short proposition: the Lord
Jehovah is an unchangeable God. However changeable forever the creatures are, yet God the Lord
changes not.

"Whoever changes, I the Lord change not. I am
always and forever the same." Now the fact that God
is unchangeable, wherein He is unchangeable, why
or whence it is that He is unchangeable, the vindication of His unchangeableness from all cavils and
objections that seem to lie against it, and the practi-
cal improvement of all this are the principal matters
that will fall under consideration in the prosecution
of this argument. And I hope that, by the assistance
of God, we shall find some light, and much comfort
and quickening, in our going through them.

Chapter Two

Which contains a general proof of the unchangeableness of God

The creatures, yes, the best of creatures in themselves are subject to change; but God is in every way, in all respects, unchangeable. God Himself expressly here (you see) asserts His own unchangeableness: "I am the Lord, I change not." It is frequently asserted also elsewhere. "Every good and perfect gift cometh down from above, from the Father of lights, with whom is no variableness or shadow of change" (James 1:17). God is here called "the Father of lights." He is sometimes called light itself: "God is light" (1 John 1:5). By this are noted to us the majesty, holiness, and perfect blessedness of God; and here He is called "the Father of lights," to note that all light, all glory, all holiness and blessedness are originally in Him, and that whatever these creatures partake of comes from Him as its proper spring and fountain.

Now with this Father of lights there is "no variableness, no mutation." The word in the Greek is an astronomical term taken from the heavenly bodies which suffer many declinations and revolutions; the heavenly lights have their vicissitude and eclipses, their decreases and increases; but with God, "the Father of lights," there is no such thing. He always shines with the same brightness, luster, and glory: "with whom is no variableness, nor shadow of turning." That is, He is without the least show or resemblance of change; nothing that looks like a change is found in Him. God is a sun which does not set and rise, that can never be overcast or eclipsed. "I said, 'O my God, take me not away in the midst of my days; Thy years are throughout all generations. Of old hast Thou laid the foundations of the earth, and the heavens are the work of Thy hands. They all perish, but Thou shalt endure, all of them shall wax old like a garment; as a vesture shalt Thou change them, and they shall be changed. But Thou art the same, and Thy years shall have no end' " (Psalm 102:24–27).

Observe that the heavens are the purest part of the creation, yet they, the psalmist tells us, "shall wax old and be changed"; but, says he to God, "Thou art the same, and Thy years shall have no end. Thou changest not, but what Thou are Thou wilt be so forever." The heavens, and so all the creatures, do not only wax old and change, but, observe, they "change and wax old like a garment." Cloth, by degrees, will rot and be eaten out by moths, but a garment or vesture is worn and wasted every day. Every day brings changes upon the creatures more or less, but God changes not. He remains the same forever. "From everlasting to everlasting He is God" (Psalm 90:2), that is, He is unchangeably one and the same infinitely holy and blessed One. "God," said one of the ancients, "who changes all things, who works all things that are in the world, is Himself unchangeable, never new, never old."

Thus you see that God is unchangeable. Now if you ask me what this unchangeableness of God is, I answer that it is that attribute of God whereby He is free from all corruption and alteration and is always like Himself, so that He can neither cease to be what He is or begin to be what He is not. And hereby He is infinitely distinguished from all the creatures in perfection and glory. They are subject to corruption and alteration, at least in their own nature, if not in their condition. They may cease to be what they are and may begin to be what they are not. They may lose what they had and attain something which before they had not; even the very angels themselves are in themselves thus mutable, as may be more fully hereafter shown. But with God there is no such thing. He is free from all possibility of corruption or alteration. He is always the same, nor can He cease to be what He is or begin to be what He is not. But that God is unchangeable, and also what His unchangeableness is, will further appear by what next falls under consideration.

Chapter Three

*Which shows wherein, in a peculiar manner,
God is unchangeable*

Having thus given you a general proof of God's unchangeableness, our next work shall be to consider wherein He is unchangeable, by which we shall be both further enlightened and confirmed in this truth and, withal, brought, I hope, into an acquaintance with the life, power, and sweetness of it, at least in some measure. God, then, is unchangeable, especially in six things, all of which carry inexpressible sweetness as well as glory in them, and should be great encouragements to our faith and comfort. He is unchangeable:

1. In His being and essence.
2. In His blessedness and glory.
3. In His counsels and decrees.
4. In His kingdom and rule.
5. In His covenant and promise.
6. In His love and grace toward His people.

1. God is unchangeable in His being and essence. What the being or essence of God is we cannot easily conceive or apprehend. The learned tell us that the essence or being of God is that one mere and pure act whereby God is God, or that God, in respect of His essence, is one most pure and mere

act from which all things are and to which all things return; that is, He is the first cause and the last end of all things. But whatever the essence or being of God is, yet, to be sure, He is therein unchangeable. He cannot be changed into another essence or being, nor can that which He has, or rather is, be corrupted or decay. So much is held further in my very text, God therein calling Himself "Jehovah," which name or title of His notes, as the truth and absoluteness, so the sameness and unchangeableness of His being. Thus Calvin and others note upon the passage, and therefore make that statement ("I change not") to be but an exegesis, or something added by way of explication, of this title "Jehovah," which God here gives Himself. "I am Jehovah, I change not. I am an absolute, independent, unchangeable being in Myself, and One who gives being to all the creatures."

And thus those learned in the Hebrew tongue all expound this glorious name of God. They tell us that this glorious name of His notes both His being and the unchangeableness of His being. And when God, as in my text, says, "I am Jehovah," He in one word says, "I am He, that great He, who has My being in and of Myself, and give being to all the creatures, and who in My being was from all eternity, am now, and will be one and the same forever."

The same thing God asserts of Himself in that other name of His, where He calls Himself "I AM." God said unto Moses, "I AM WHAT I AM." And He said, "Thus shalt thou say unto the children of Israel, 'I AM hath sent me unto you' " (Exodus 3:14). "I AM WHAT I AM," or "I will what I will be," notes

eternal and unchangeable being in Himself, and
that He is now and will be forever that which He was
before to Abraham, Isaac, and Jacob. It notes the necessity, eternity, immutability, and infinite fullness
of God's being, and indeed that the fountain of all
being is in Him. It declares Him to be perpetually
God, and to this name Christ alluded when He asserted His own divinity: "Before Abraham was, I Am"
(John 8:58). Also, "Thou art the same" (Psalm
102:27), says the psalmist to God, or, which is more
suitable to the Hebrew, "Thou art Thyself, always
Thyself." Thus God is unchangeable in His being or
essence; and when I say He is unchangeable in His
being or essence, I say He is unchangeable in all His
essential properties: His wisdom, His power, His justice, His holiness, His omniscience, His all-sufficiency, and the like. For mark, the attributes or
properties of God are not in Him distinguished either from His essence or from one another really,
but only as we perceive them; that is, they are not
distinguished at all in God, but are all one and the
same perfection in Him. They are indeed, as was
noted in the beginning, the divine essence itself according to this general rule: whatever is in God is
God. They are distinguished only in the manner of
our understanding which, being unable to compre-
hend that infinite pure act at once, conceives
thereof after the manner of many acts. So I say, when
we affirm that God is unchangeable in His being or
essence, we affirm that He is unchangeable in all
His attributes and perfections, in His holiness, His
wisdom, His power, His greatness, His love, and the
like. I will close this section with a great saying

which I have read in Augustine: "Thou (says he to God) alone are God, that being which cannot possibly be changed, either into a better or worse being, because Thou art a most simple being," to whom "It is not one thing to live, and another thing to live blessedly, and that because Thou art Thine own blessedness."

2. God is unchangeable in His blessedness and glory. The Lord Jehovah is a glorious and blessed God, "the blessed and only Potentate" (1 Timothy 6:15). He is blessed, and that not only objectively, as He is the great object of the praises, blessings, and admiration of men and angels forever, nor only as He is the spring and fountain of all that blessedness which the one and the other of them eternally enjoy, but subjectively, being a God infinitely blessed and happy. God is the most happy and blessed being. He is so blessed that it is more than all the creatures, whether men or angels, can do to add the least tittle or iota to His blessedness. Hence we read that "their goodness extendeth not to Him" (Psalm 16:2). And again, "Can a man be profitable unto God? And is it gain to Him that thou makest thy ways perfect?" (Job 22:2–3). That is, it is no profit, no gain to God, no addition to His happiness or perfection, that we, or any, are or do certain things. See also Job 35:7–8: "If thou be righteous, what givest thou unto Him? Or what receivest He of thine hand? Thy wickedness may hurt a man as thou art, and thy righteousness may profit the son of man, but not God." It is as if he should say, "God is never the more happy or unhappy by anything the creature does or

can do." It is true that the saints and angels both love Him, praise Him, admire and adore Him forever; they cast all their crowns down at His foot. But alas! This adds not one iota to His happiness; no, "He is exalted above all blessing and praise" (Nehemiah 9:5). Yes, it is a stooping, a condescension in Him to take notice of these things, as described in Psalm 113:5–6. And, indeed, it is our happiness, not God's, to love Him, serve Him, praise Him, walk with Him, and live to Him. "Who art Thou, Lord," said Augustine, "and what am I that Thou shouldst command me to love Thee, that Thou will accept love from me, and threaten me with great miseries unless I will love Thee?" He admires the condescension of God herein.

Yes, such is the blessedness of God that He Himself cannot add hereunto. God cannot make Himself more blessed, happy, and perfect than He is; nothing can by infiniteness be added unto infiniteness. Now as He is thus blessed, so His blessedness is unchangeable; hence one of His names is "over all, God blessed for evermore" (Romans 9:5), throughout all ages, and to all eternity. Alas! God makes His people unchangeably blessed, and He who makes others unchangeably blessed is doubtless unchangeable in His own blessedness.

But this will further appear by considering a little what the blessedness of God is and wherein it lies. It lies wholly in that infinite delight, solace, and satisfaction which He has in Himself, in the vision and fruition of Himself and those infinite glories and perfections which are in Him, and which

He sees and knows will be in Him forever. First, God is an infinite ocean of sweetness, perfection, and glory. He has all good and all perfection in Him, as in its fountain, fullness, and purity. As all the lines in the circumference meet and are united in the center, so all excellencies and perfections meet and are united in God, as God has all excellencies and perfections in Him.

Second, He perfectly understands His own infinite perfections, contemplates them, and has an infinite delight, solace, and satisfaction in them. He is infinitely pleased and at rest in Himself, and in the vision and fruition of His own perfections; this is His blessedness. Hence He tells us that He is God all-sufficient; that is, for and to Himself, as well as for and to His people: "I am God all-sufficient. I am My own blessedness," and to Abraham, "I am your blessedness, and I have enough for both."

The truth is, all our happiness lies in God, in the knowledge and enjoyment of God. "This is life eternal, to know Thee, the only true God" (John 17:3). "Happy is that people whose God is the Lord" (Psalm 144:15). "He that made me is good," said Augustine, "and He is my good, my happiness, and in Him will I exult and rejoice above all my other good things." And it is a great saying which he has to the same purpose elsewhere: "Unhappy is that man who knows all other things, but is ignorant of Thee, O God; but blessed is he who knows Thee, though he is ignorant of other things. But he who knows both Thee and other things too, he is not the more happy because he knows other things, but he is happy in Thee only."

Thus our happiness lies in God, and the vision of Him; and where should His own happiness lie but in Himself? He who is the spring and fountain of our happiness is an everlasting fountain of happiness to Himself. "Thou Thyself," said Augustine, "art Thine own happiness."

I will close this section with a great saying of a learned man: "God is such an infinitely perfect and happy being that nothing can be added to Him, nothing can be taken from Him. He can want nothing out of Himself, nor can He receive anything but from Himself; and He is infinitely sufficient for and to Himself, having all things in Himself."

3. God is unchangeable in His counsels and decrees. We read in Scripture several times of the counsels of God: "Thy counsels of old are faithfulness and truth" (Isaiah 25:1), and He is said "to work all things according to the counsel of His own will" (Ephesians 1:11). And the same thing is elsewhere mentioned under the notion sometimes of His purpose and sometimes His decree. To understand this, you must know that God, from all eternity, did, as it were, sit in council with His own wisdom, justice, and grace, and in that council did absolutely decree and determine the futurition, that is to say, the infallible future being of whatever is besides Himself, unto the praise of His own glory. That is the purpose, counsel, or decree of God: it is His free, absolute, and eternal determining of all things which have been, are, or shall be as He saw fit to have them; or it is that one, free, constant act of God whereby He has absolutely determined all things in

subservience to His own glory.

Now in this counsel or decree of His, He is unchangeable and the same forever. What He wills, He wills always, His willing of things being one pure act without any interruption or shadow of change. Of this the Scripture is full: "The counsel of the Lord standeth forever, the thoughts of His heart to all generations" (Psalm 33:11). "There are many devices in a man's heart; nevertheless the counsel of the Lord, that shall stand" (Proverbs 19:21). Men may plot and fight against God and His counsel, but yet it will stand, and that forever. And you have this truth asserted by God Himself, you have it from His own mouth: "My counsel shall stand, and I will do all My pleasure" (Isaiah 46:10). God derides the counsels of men who oppose Him and His people, telling them expressly that they shall not stand (Isaiah 8:10). But as for His own counsel, that shall stand; hence also we read of the immutability of His counsel, "God willing more abundantly to show unto the heirs of promise the immutability of His counsel, confirmed it by an oath, that by two immutable things, wherein it was impossible for God to lie, we might have strong consolation" (Hebrews 6:17–18). Mark, "the immutability of His counsel," and "two immutable things wherein it was impossible for God to lie." That is, His counsel and His oath, and His counsel is confirmed by His oath—confirmed, namely, to our faith, not in itself, for His counsel in itself is as firm without as with His oath, and His oath is added merely as an indulgence and condescension to our weakness. Therefore it is added that "we might have strong consolation," and it is "to show unto the heirs of promise."

As His counsels in general, so also His particular counsels concerning men's eternal states are immutable. "The foundation of God standeth sure, having this seal: the Lord knoweth who are His" (2 Timothy 2:19). He shows it here by the metaphor of both a foundation and seal. Here is to be understood God's decree of election unto eternal life; and this "standeth sure," says the Apostle; this changes not, this varies not. And to the same purpose Calvin speaks upon the passage: "The Apostle calls us to look back upon the election of God, which he calls a foundation, hereby showing the firm and stable constancy or immutability of it." We read "that the purpose of God according to election might stand" (Romans 9:11). God will have His own eternal purpose according to His election stand, and stand it shall, and that forever. Thus God is unchangeable in His counsels. Alas! All His counsels are free, wise, and absolute, powerful counsels, and therefore they cannot change. And this Calvin takes to be a special part of the meaning of the text; namely, God's unchangeableness in His counsels, for thus he speaks. "God (says Calvin) remains firm and steadfast in His own purposes, nor is He bent or varied this way and that way, as men oftentimes repent of and change their own counsels because things come into their mind which they thought not of before; and so they undo that which they have done, and seek ways of retracting their own acts." I have read this in Augustine, "God changes His works, not His counsels." Oh, let us reverence and adore God in this His unchangeableness!

4. God is unchangeable in His kingdom and rule. God has a kingdom and dominion over the whole world, which kingdom and dominion of His is that absolute right and power whereby He possesses all things as His own and also orders and disposes of them as He pleases, ruling and governing the whole world according to the counsel of His own will, and in a subservience to His own most wise and holy ends. Hence He is said to be "over all" (Romans 9:5), and "above all" (Ephesians 4:6), to wit, in kingdom, power, and dominion. He has a right to all, and He has the right to order and dispose of all, both persons and things, states and kingdoms. "He is the most high, that ruleth in the kingdoms of men, and gives them to whomsoever He will" (Daniel 4:32). He works all and orders all in the kingdom of providence, as well as in the kingdom of grace, and that "according to the counsel of His own will" (Ephesians 1:11). He rules and commands all. "He hath prepared His throne in the heavens, and His kingdom ruleth over all" (Psalm 103:19). "He does whatsoever He pleases in heaven and on earth, in the seas, and in all deep places" (Psalm 135:6).

Now in this kingdom and dominion of His, He is unchangeable; it admits of neither stop nor period; He rules by His power forever. "Thy kingdom, O Lord, is an everlasting kingdom, a kingdom of ages, and Thy dominion endureth throughout all generations" (Psalm 145:13). "And I blessed the most High (says Nebuchadnezzar), whose dominion is an everlasting dominion, and His kingdom from generation to generation" (Daniel 4:34). Whatever men

think, yet God governs the world and His dominion
is over all. "The Lord reigns" (Psalm 93:1). He has
reigned, He does reign, and He will reign forever.
"There is a day coming when all rule, authority, and
power shall be put down" (1 Corinthians 15:24), and
that once for all, even the principality of the angels
themselves (as Calvin observes) not excepted. But
God reigns forever and ever and His kingdom has
no end. Thus He is unchangeable in His kingdom
and rule in the world, which is a great encouragement to the people of God.

O my beloved! God governs the world now as well
as heretofore, yes, and He governs it in our nature
now as well as heretofore (John 5:27). He governs all
by the man Christ, who has a natural, tender care of,
and respect to, His church and people in all. Let us
therefore say with the psalmist, "The Lord reigneth,
let the people tremble; the Lord reigneth, let Zion
rejoice." God is not, God cannot be taken from His
throne and kingdom.

5. God is unchangeable in His covenant and
promise with His people in Christ. God has made a
covenant with His people in Christ, a covenant of
peace, a covenant of grace, a covenant of love, a
covenant founded upon grace, a covenant full of
grace, a covenant wholly made up of grace and love
from first to last, therefore called grace in the abstract (Romans 6:14), a full covenant, a rich
covenant, a precious covenant, a covenant made up
of rich, yes, exceedingly rich and precious promises,
and filled with exceedingly rich and precious treasures, precious grace, precious peace, precious par-

don, precious righteousness, precious salvation, with a precious God, a precious Christ, a precious Spirit, a precious heaven and blessedness forever. Now in this covenant, and in all precious promises of it, is God the Lord unchangeable? Hence you have it so often called an everlasting covenant: "I will establish My covenant between Me and thee (said God to Abraham) for an everlasting covenant, to be a God unto thee, and to thy seed after thee" (Genesis 17:7). Again, "I will make an everlasting covenant with them, (speaking of His people) and I will not turn from them to do them good" (Jeremiah 32:40).

As it is an everlasting covenant, so it is an everlasting and sure covenant. "God hath made with me an everlasting covenant (says David), well ordered in all things, and sure" (2 Samuel 23:5). And again, "Come and I will make with you an everlasting covenant, even the sure mercies of David" (Isaiah 55:3). Hence also it is called "a covenant of salt" (Numbers 18:19), that is, a firm, a durable, an unchangeable covenant. In many other ways God sets forth the immutability of His covenant, and that for the encouragement of our faith and comfort. How sweet is that word, and what a rest may it be to faith! " 'This is as the waters of Noah unto me; for as I have sworn that the waters of Noah should no more go over the earth, so have I sworn that I will no more be wroth with thee, nor rebuke thee. For the mountains shall depart, and the hills be removed, but My kindness shall not depart from thee, neither shall the covenant of My peace be removed,' saith the Lord, that hath mercy on thee" (Isaiah 54:9–10).

Observe, God had in the two foregoing verses promised His church and people that though for a small moment He had forsaken them, yet with great mercies He would gather them; and that though in a little wrath He had hidden His face from them for a moment, yet with everlasting kindness He would have mercy on them. And here, in these two verses, He gives them a double ground of the assurance hereof: the one taken from His oath and the unchangeableness thereof (verse 9), the other from His covenant, and the unchangeableness thereof (verse 10): "For the mountains shall depart," as if He should say, "The mountains and hills may sooner be removed than My covenant. Yes, the time will come when these shall be removed, but the time will never come that My covenant shall fail or be removed."

But what if His people sin, what then? Why, then, He will correct and chastise them for their sin, but His covenant He will keep firm and inviolable forever notwithstanding. For this you have a full and clear text: "If his children forsake My law, and walk not in My judgements; if they break My statutes, and keep not My commandments; then will I visit their transgressions with a rod, and their iniquities with stripes. Nevertheless (oh, gracious nevertheless!) My loving kindness will I not take from him, nor suffer My faithfulness to fail; My covenant will I not break" (Psalm 89:30–34). We sin and break, and break and sin; and God chastises us, it may be, for our sin, but yet His covenant remains firm and unchangeable. "If we believe not, yet He abideth faithful, He cannot deny Himself" (2 Timothy 2:13).

"Oh, I have an unbelieving heart, and I shall, I

fear, forfeit all." Although you have an unbelieving heart, yet God remains faithful. Thus God is unchangeable in His covenant. Alas, His covenant is built upon unchangeable love, and sealed with unchangeable blood, and cannot therefore but be unchangeable! And as the covenant, so all the promises of the covenant are sure and unchangeable: "they are all Yea and Amen, in Christ" (2 Corinthians 1:20), that is, they are all sure, firm, unchangeable promises, promises that will certainly be made good. Men promise many times and change, but God promises and changes not; and this some conceive to be held forth in that name of His, "I AM" (Exodus 3:14). "I AM WHAT I AM," or, "I am what I was," or, "I will be what I was." That is, as one expounds, "I will be in My performances what I was in My promises." God makes good all His promises to a tittle. He who is truth itself and faithfulness itself cannot lie, cannot fail. It is a sweet saying I have read in Augustine: "They are Thy promises, O Lord, and who need fear being deceived when truth itself promises?" Oh, we need not fear, we need not question, for God is true, God is faithful! Oh, how sweet are the thoughts of an unchangeable covenant! God has laid Himself under bonds to His people when He was infinitely free in Himself, and under bonds to do great things for them, to pardon their iniquities, transgressions and sins; to give them a new heart and a new spirit; to pour out His Spirit upon them; to cause them to walk in His statutes and judgments to do them; to write His laws in their hearts and put them into their inward parts; to cleanse them from all their filthiness and idols; to put His fear into their hearts that they shall never depart from Him; and (which is all in one) to be a God unto them, and that they shall be His people; that is, He has laid Himself under bonds to be to them and to do for them what a God can be to and do for them. He is firm and unchangeable in all, and all shall assuredly have its accomplishment in its season. Oh, how sweet is this! This was David's deathbed comfort: "Although my house be not so with God, yet He hath made me an everlasting covenant; and this is all my salvation and all my desire" (2 Samuel 23:5). And, indeed, well it might be, for what could David or anyone desire more than is contained in God's covenant, which has heaven and earth, God and the creature, time and eternity, all in it? Oh, study this covenant of God, and the unchangeableness of it, and you will find it an unchangeable spring of comfort to you! God Himself found fault with the first covenant, it is said, and why? Because it made no provision for His people against sin; but you will be able to find no fault with this covenant, this being well ordered in all things and sure.

6. God is unchangeable in His grace and love toward His people. God loves His people, and that with a choice and peculiar love, a love like that wherewith He loves Christ Himself (John 17:23). They are indeed the "dearly beloved of His soul" (Jeremiah 12:7), and in this love of His towards them He is unchangeable, always the same, which I shall at once a little open and evince unto you in three propositions.

(1) God is unchangeable in His love itself for His people, that being always the same towards them. "I have loved thee with an everlasting love" (Jeremiah 31:3), with a love that is from everlasting to everlasting, without change or period. God's love for His people is so firm and stable that nothing whatever can possibly nullify or alter it; nothing can possibly cast them out of His heart. If anything could do it, it would be their sinning against Him and their breaking with Him; but these do not, cannot do it, so He has told us: "If they sin, I will correct them for their sin; but My lovingkindness I will not take from them" (Psalm 89:30–33); or (as some render it) "I will not so much as interpret My love towards them," as if He should say, "Though they sin, yet I'll love them still."

God does not love the sins of His people; no, He hates them, but He loves their persons notwithstanding their sins. But what if afflictions and temptations are added to their sins, and both the one and the other rise high; will not this break off His love from them? No, see that triumph of the Apostle on this account: "Who shall separate us from the love of God; shall tribulation, or distress or persecution, and the like? Nay, in all these things we are more than conquerors, through Him that loved us; for I am persuaded that neither death, nor life, nor angels, nor principalities, nor powers, nor things present, nor things to come, nor height nor depth, nor any other creature shall be able to separate us from the love of God which is in Christ Jesus our Lord" (Romans 8:35, 37–39). Here you see are afflictions and temptations added to sins; yes, here are heights and depths of these things, but all cannot separate God's people from His love, nor cast them out of His heart. One I remember gives the sum of the whole in this short word: "God has loved from eternity, and He will love to eternity." The truth is, if either sins or sufferings could cast us out of God's heart and separate us from His love, who then among the saints could hope to continue in His love and upon His heart? Besides, in the words previously quoted from Isaiah 54:9–10, God says expressly "that though the mountains should be removed, yet His kindness to His people should not be removed; no, that remains firm and steadfast forever."

True, God may possibly afflict His people, and that in many ways, and very sorely. He may speak against them as against Ephraim (Jeremiah 31:20) He may write against them, and that with bitter things, as against Job (Job 13:26). He may fight against them, as against those in Isaiah 63:10. He may frown upon them, and let in His terrors into them, as He did upon and into Heman (Psalm 88), but yet still He loves them; still they are dear to Him.

(2) God is unchangeable in all the special saving fruits and effects of His love toward His people. "The gifts and calling of God are without repentance" (Romans 11:29). That is, the gifts of His effectual calling, or His saving gifts, such as effectual calling and the like, shall never be repented of, never be recalled or reversed by Him. As they who receive those gifts will have no cause to repent, but to rejoice in them forever, so God who gives them will not repent that He gave them to them. God gives Christ. He gives grace. He gives peace. He gives

pardon. He gives righteousness. He gives salvation. He gives eternal life to His people, and all out of His love toward them. And He never recalls or reverses the fruits and effects of love. You have another full text for this: "Every good and every perfect gift is from above, and cometh down from the Father of lights, with whom is no variableness nor shadow of turning" (James 1:17). Notice, having spoken of the perfect gifts of God, presently he adds "with whom is no variableness," as if He should say, "As all good and saving gifts come from God, so He is unchangeable in all."

Indeed there are common gifts, and gifts of a mere outward calling, which God, out of a common love and bounty, gives to men; and these many times He recalls, they not improving them. So the talent was taken from the slothful servant (Matthew 25:28), and you know what Christ spoke immediately thereupon: "Unto everyone that hath shall be given, and he shall have abundance; but from him that hath not, shall be taken away, even that which he hath" (Matthew 25:29). Pray observe, "To him that hath shall be given," that is, whoever God has bestowed gifts and talents upon, if he improves them for God and his own salvation, he shall have more gifts and more talents. He shall have an abundant increase of these things, "but from him that hath not shall be taken away even that which he hath." Here seems to be a contradiction: "him that hath not," and yet "what he has." The meaning in short is this: when God bestows such and such gifts and talents upon a person to be employed for His glory, and he does not so employ them, he does not rightly use and improve them, what God has bestowed upon him shall be taken away. But it is otherwise with the saving gifts and fruits of God's special love. These God never recalls, which is a sweet contemplation. Soul! Has God bestowed some of His saving gifts upon you? Then they are yours forever. Has He given you His Christ? He will never repent of it, never call Him back again, but sweet Jesus is yours forever. Has He given you His Spirit? He will never repent of it, nor will He ever recall this blessed gift from you; the holy, good, and glorious Spirit is yours forever. Has He given you a new and spiritual life? Has He given you grace, pardon, righteousness, justification, and the like? He will never repent of it; all these are yours forever. Oh, how sweet is this to contemplate! You may sit down and say, "Christ is mine; the Comforter is mine; life, peace, pardon, righteousness, salvation are all mine, and that forever."

(3) God is unchangeable in the real designs and workings of His love (I say real, though not sensible). God's love toward His people may be suspended and interrupted, as to the sensible influences and manifestations thereof, but yet even then it is active and really at work for them; however, the outward dispensation may vary—now a smile, then a frown; now lifted up, then cast down; now full, then empty; now light, then darkness. Yet, in all, still He goes on in one even, constant tenure of love towards them. In all, His love is at work for them and towards them, and He intends and designs them as much love in one as in the other, and accordingly first or last effects and accomplishes it. And this is but agreeable to His covenant with them and

promise to them: "I will make (says He to His people) an everlasting covenant with you, never to turn
away from you to do you good" (Jeremiah 32:40), and
"All things shall work together for good to them
that love God" (Romans 8:28).

Whatever God does with us, however He seems to
carry it towards us, yet still He is doing us good and
acting out His love towards us. "We (as a holy man
speaks) are apt to think that God shows us love
when He does some great thing for us; but God is
always acting out His love towards us, when He
frowns as well as when He smiles; when He with-
draws as well as when He approaches to us."

In a word, soul, whatever God does, there is love
in it, and He designs your love and good by it. Does
He smile, give full, keep alive, draw near to you? In
all there is love, His special love works and runs
through all. Or does He frown, take, empty, kill,
hide His face? In all this there is love; yes, the same
special love of His works in all and runs through all.
God is acting out of His love toward you in the one
as well as in the other. Oh, how sweet is this! Death
to the people of God comes from the same fountain
of love in God's heart as life.

Chapter Four

*Which gives an account why or whence
it is that God is unchangeable*

That God is unchangeable you have already seen. That which falls next under consideration is to show whence it is that God is indeed thus unchangeable; or, if you will, what basis and foundation the unchangeableness of God is built upon. It is built upon a threefold basis or foundation:

1. The infinite purity and simplicity of His nature.
2. The infinite excellency and perfection of His being.
3. The infinite extent and compass of His wisdom.

1. The unchangeableness of God is built upon, or springs from, the infinite purity and simplicity of His nature. God is a most pure act. He is a Spirit, an infinite Spirit (John 4:24), and so an infinitely pure, simple, uncompounded Being, and therefore unchangeable. "God is a most simply and perfectly pure act, free from all composition, and therefore cannot possibly be dissolved, corrupted, or wax old and decay." And Augustine, I remember, grounds God's unchangeableness upon this ground or basis:

"Thou only art God and cannot be changed, either into a better or worse being than what Thou art, because Thou art a most pure and simple Being." Men, and so other creatures, have their mixtures and compositions; they are made up of different elements, qualities, and humors, and that is one reason among others why they change; but God is a most pure and simple Being. He is purity and simplicity itself, and therefore unchangeable. Angels and souls have a composition in them; they are compounded of subject and accidents, nature and qualities, or graces; but God is one mere and perfect act, without all composition, division, multiplication, or the like and therefore without change. Where there is composition, there may be mutation; but where there is infinite simplicity, there is absolute immutability, and thus it is, you see, with God.

2. The unchangeableness of God is built upon, and arises from, the infinite excellency and perfection of His being. As God is a most pure and simple act, so He is a most perfect Being, an infinitely perfect Being, and therefore unchangeable. Men are imperfect, and therefore they change. God is perfect, and therefore He changes not. All change argues imperfection in the subject changed. For, pray observe, there is a twofold change: there is a corruptive change and there is a perfective change. A corruptive change is a change from good to bad or from bad to worse; and such a change, to be sure, argues imperfection in the subject. A perfective change is a change from bad to good or from good to better; and this also argues imperfection in the subject. This argues the subject to be imperfect be-

fore, whatever it is now. Thus all change necessarily argues imperfection; but God is infinitely perfect, and therefore not subject to change. He is capable of no corruptive change, nor a perfective change, because He is an infinitely perfect Being, and so can have nothing added to Him, nothing taken from Him. "Be ye perfect (says Christ) as your heavenly Father is perfect" (Matthew 5:48). Our heavenly Father is a perfect Being. He is both essentially and originally perfect. He is perfect in Himself, having all excellencies and perfections centering in Him; and He is the spring and cause of all those excellencies and perfections that are found in the creatures. "God is light, and in Him is no darkness at all" (1 John 1:5), that is, He is both pure and perfect—pure without mixture and perfect without defect. He is wholly perfection, and therefore unchangeable. What shall I say? God is so good, so full, so blessed, so perfect in every way that it is impossible He should change. It is a great speech I have read in one of the ancients: "For Thou, or to Thee, Lord, to be and to live, are not two things; because Thou art the chief Being, and the chief Life. Thou are every way, the highest, the chiefest, the most excellent, and Thou are not changed." And indeed, therefore, He cannot change. God has told us that He is all-sufficient: "I am God almighty, God all-sufficient. I have all fullness, blessedness and perfection in Me."

"He (as one upon this passage notes) is most sufficient, One who is infinitely sufficient for Himself, and who also vouchsafes a sufficiency to His people." He has all excellency and perfection in Him, and that in a blessed union and conjunction; and how then should He change?

3. The unchangeableness of God is built upon, and springs from, the infinite fullness and extent of His wisdom and understanding. As God is a most pure and perfect act, so He is a most wise Being, and therefore unchangeable. And this refers principally to His unchangeableness in His kingdom, counsels, covenant, and love. Men's wisdom is weak and their understandings dark and shallow, and therefore they change. They are not today what they were yesterday, nor will they be tomorrow, perhaps, what they are today; but God is infinitely wise and knows all things, and therefore He changes not. He is the same forever. "Men change (said Calvin); they oftentimes wish the things undone which they have done, and seek ways of retracting their own acts or grants, because with them things come to mind many times which they foresaw not, nor ever thought of; but God denies any such thing to be found with Him. He is infinitely wise. He has a perfect knowledge and understanding of things, and therefore changes not."

He is called in Scripture "a God of knowledge" (1 Samuel 2:3). Yes, He is said to be "perfect in knowledge" (Job 37:16). He has a perfect knowledge of all things, whether past, present, or to come. He sees and knows all things at once, with one prospect or by one single aspect, and that unerringly and infallibly. He knows all things by one most simple, immutable, and eternal act of understanding. God is in Scripture called "the only wise God" (1 Timothy 1: 17), and His understanding is said to be infinite (Psalm 147:5). God sees and knows Himself and in

Himself, all things, always, perfectly, and at once; all things, without exception, always without interruption; perfectly without defect, and at once without succession. "Known unto God are all His works from the foundation of the world," says the Apostle in Acts 15:18. In a word, God has a perfect prospect of all things in His eternity. Neither can there be anything new to Him that should occasion a change in Him. And thus you see upon what basis or foundation the unchangeableness of God is built.

Chapter Five

Several propositions laid down for the obviating of objections, and the vindication of God's unchangeableness from all cavil and contradiction

The next work we have to do is to vindicate the unchangeableness of God from all cavil and contradiction, and to obviate such objections as may seem to lie against it, which I shall do by making good these four propositions:

1. God's repenting, which we sometimes read of in Scripture, is no way inconsistent with or repugnant to the truth and glory of His unchangeableness. Oftentimes in Scripture God is said to repent, both of what He has done and of what He has said He would do. First, He is said to repent of some things He had done. So He is said "to repent that ever He made man" (Genesis 6:6). It repented the Lord that He had made man on the earth; and it grieved Him at His heart. So it repented Him that He had made Saul king. "It repenteth me (said God) that I have set up Saul to be king" (1 Samuel 15:11).

Second, God is said to repent of some things which He had said He would do. "The Lord will repent Himself concerning His servants" (Psalm 135:14). "The Lord repented Him of the evil which He had pronounced against them" (Jeremiah 26:19). And there are many other places which might be mentioned. Thus God is said to repent in both ways. Now repentance imports a change, and how then is God unchangeable?

I answer, He is nevertheless unchangeable despite His repenting; for, pray observe: when God is said in Scripture to repent, it is to be understood not in a proper, but in an improper and allusive tense; not affective, but effective; not according to His internal will, but an external work. God is therefore said to repent because He does as men do when they repent, that is, He changes His deeds, yet without any change of His will. Yes, the change of His deeds is the execution of His unchangeable will. When men repent, they cease to do what they had begun, and they are ready to destroy what they had wrought; and thus God is said to repent not because His mind is changed, but because He ceases to do what He did, or He destroys what He had made. Thus He is said "to repent of His making Saul king," because He meant to remove him from being king, and "to repent of His making man," because He meant to destroy man for His sin.

Now such repenting does not argue the least change in God, and therefore in the very same chapter where He is said thus to repent He is also said not to repent. In 1 Samuel 15:11 He is said "to repent of making Saul king," but in verse 29 it is said of Him "that He will not lie, nor repent, nor is He a man that He should repent." He can no more repent in a proper sense, as repentance imports change, than He can lie; and when, as in verse 29 it is said of Him that "He is not a man that He should repent," there is implied that He must cease to be God and become man if He so repents as to note change in Him. It is a good, and indeed a great, observation which one has upon this passage: "No repentance can properly befall God whereas He is immutable, most wise, most blessed; but He is said to repent when He retracts and revokes His benefits from a person or people." In a word, He is said to repent as to the change of effects, but not as to Himself in either His nature or will. But this will appear further in the next proposition.

2. The non-execution and non-accomplishment of some threats and promises of God, which we find in His Word, is no impeachment of His unchangeableness. True, there are many things both threatened and promised by God in His Word that never come to pass. God sometimes threatens what He does not execute, as in the cases of Hezekiah (2 Kings 20:1, 5) and Nineveh (Jonah 3:4, 10). On the other hand, God sometimes promises that which is never accomplished, of which instances not a few might be given. Now does not this impeach and contradict His unchangeableness? I answer, "No." Neither the one nor the other of these is in any way repugnant or contradictory thereunto.

For, pray consider, those threatenings and promises which are not accomplished are not absolute, but conditional threatenings and promises, threatenings and promises that have either an express or implicit condition in them, which condition being wanting the non-accomplishment of the threat or promise is so far from being inconsistent with the unchangeableness of God that it strongly argues for it.

I shall illustrate this by one passage: "At which instant I shall speak concerning a nation, and concerning a kingdom, to pluck up, and to pull down, and to destroy it, if that nation, against whom I have pronounced, turn from their evil, I will repent of the evil that I thought to do unto them. And at what instant I shall speak concerning a nation, and concerning a kingdom, to build and to plant it, if it do evil in My sight, that it obey not My voice, then I will repent of the good wherewith I said I would benefit them" (Jeremiah 18:7–10).

Mark, here is both evil threatened and good promised, but both under a condition. Now if the condition upon which the one is threatened and the other is promised is wanting, let it not be imputed to any change in God if either the one or the other be not accomplished. When an evil is threatened and not executed, and when a good is promised and not performed, the non-execution of the one and the non-performance of the other are not because God is not unchangeable, but because the condition upon which the one was threatened or the other promised is found wanting. I might argue in like manner from Psalm 7:12, Luke 13:1–5, and Revelation 2:20–22. But let this one suffice instead of all the rest. And to this purpose speaks a learned man: "God changes His sentence, the outward threat or promise, but not His decree, not His inward counsel or purpose." And to the same effect is the saying of another: "If we respect the counsel of God, that He does not, He cannot change; but His mind and will revealed by the prophets, that is often changed." And it is a great saying of one of the schoolmen: "It is one thing for God to change His will, and another thing to will a change." God often wills and determines a change, but He never changes His will or determination. Thus, where an evil is threatened or a good promised which is not accomplished, the non-accomplishment of it is not because God is not unchangeable, but because the threat or promise was conditional, and the condition thereof was wanting.

3. None of those changes which seem to be attributed to God in Scripture are really opposed to His unchangeableness. I grant that the Scripture several times represents God as seeming, at least, to change in this relation to us. Sometimes He is represented as being changed from an enemy to a friend, to be reconciled to those with whom He was offended before. Hence we read of His "being pacified toward sinners" (Ezekiel 16:63). So, "Though Thou wast angry with me (says the church to God), yet Thine anger is turned away" (Isaiah 12:1).

Again, sometimes God is represented as being changed from a friend to an enemy, to be at war with those with whom He was before at peace. "Thou art become cruel to me" (Job 30:21), or, "Thou art turned or changed." "Thou wert good and gracious, but now Thou art severe and cruel." "He was turned to be their enemy, and fought against them" (Isaiah 63:10). Thus, in both these ways God seems to be represented as changing, and how then is He unchangeable? Nevertheless He is unchangeable in all this, and to vindicate God's unchangeableness notwithstanding this, I would entreat you to consider two things:

(1) Consider that God is unchangeable under the most various and changeable dispensations that He does or can walk in towards us. It is true, the external dispensation changes. His outward course and carriage towards us is very changeable and various: now He smiles and then He frowns; now He fills and then He empties; now He lifts up and then He casts down; now He breaks and then He binds up. Thus the outward dealings and dispensations of God are very changeable and various; yet in and under all He Himself changes not, but is still the same—the same in His being and in His blessedness, the same in His counsel, covenant, and love toward us. Hence, "All the paths (that is, the providences and dispensations) of the Lord" are said to be "mercy and truth to His people" (Psalm 25:10). His paths towards them are very various in themselves, but God's love and grace are all the same in all. The outward dispensation of God toward us, it may be, is changed. He smiled, but now He frowns. He gave, but now He takes away. He formed light, but now He creates darkness for us. And hereupon we apprehend that God Himself—His heart, His counsel, His covenant, His love—is changed. But it is only in our apprehension, for indeed, and in truth, He is the same still. The most variable of His dispensations do not argue the least variableness in Him at all; and indeed, where He is a friend, He is a friend forever; where He is an enemy, He is an enemy forever. The change is only in the external dispensation.

(2) Consider that the change is in us and not in God. God is always the same, but we are not the

same. When God is pacified towards those with
whom He was offended, they are changed, not He.
He is the same as He was. And when He is angry
with saints with whom He was before at peace, they
are changed, not He. The change was in Job, not in
God, when he said, "Thou art turned to be cruel to
me." The change was in the church, not in God,
when He was said "to be turned to be their enemy."

"God (says a worthy divine) is the same. His love
is the same. His wrath is the same. His mercy is the
same. His justice is the same, and that forever; but
we, changing, are cast sometimes under the effects
of His love and sometimes under the effects of His
wrath. We are sometimes under the saddest droppings of His justice, and sometimes under the
sweetest influences of His mercy."

If a man changes his direction, and turns his
body to face another point of the heavens, that part
of the heavens which was before at his right hand is
now at his left. The heavens are still as they were;
they change not, either their position or motion,
but the man has changed his. So the wrath and love,
the justice and mercy of God stand always at the
same point, but we turn, sometimes justice-ward,
sometimes mercy-ward. Now we face His wrath, and
then we face His love. Thus the change is in us and
not in God, and so He remains unchangeable still.

4. God's unchangeableness in no way excludes or
invalidates the use of means. If God is unchangeable, one might ask, then to what purpose is the use
of means? Why do we pray, hear, or use any means in
order to our eternal good? Why, God's unchangeableness does not in any way exclude or invalidate

the use of means; for pray, consider, first, that God wills the means as well as the end, and the means in order *to* the end. He wills our praying as well as our pardon, our hearing as well as our happiness, our sowing as well as our reaping, our sowing in the use of means as well as our reaping in the harvest of mercy. He wills our believing as well as our blessedness. He wills the one as well as the other; yes, He wills the one in order to lead to the other, and that with the same absolute, immutable, and eternal will. "He hath ordained we should walk in good works" (Ephesians 2:10), and "He hath chosen us to salvation, through the sanctification of the Spirit, and the belief of the truth" (2 Thessalonians 2:13).

Second, consider that as God wills the means as well as the end, so it is through the use of these that He gives out of Himself and His blessings to us, and at last brings us to the end. God makes a covenant with His people, and therein lays Himself under bonds to do great things for them, as great as a God can do. But He will have them pray for them, nor will He do them but in a way of prayer (Ezekiel 36:37). God tells us that "I never said to the seed of Jacob, 'Seek ye Me in vain' " (Isaiah 45:19).

Indeed, God is not wanting to His people in the use of means. "The Lord is good to them that wait for Him, to the soul that seeks Him" (Lamentations 3:25). Ordinarily God will not communicate Himself and His love in any other way; and the soul that neglects this puts himself out of the way of the manifestations and communications of God and His love. Indeed, God has, as it were, tied Himself to souls under a conscientious use of means to do them good: "Ask, and you shall receive; seek, and you shall find; knock, and it shall be opened to you. For everyone that asketh, receiveth; and everyone that seeketh, findeth; and to him that knocketh, it is opened" (Matthew 7:7–8). As you therefore value communion with God, and the manifestations of His love, take heed of laying aside the use of means.

Third, consider that these things we call means (such as prayer, hearing, and the like) are instances of our homage, worship, and obedience to God. Hereby we worship God, and give so far the glory to Him that is due unto His name. And consequently, to cast off these is to cast off the worship of God and to deny that we owe homage to Him.

Lay all these together and our proposition is clear: God's unchangeableness does not in any way exclude or invalidate the use of means. And when we use means it is not to change, but to fulfill the mind of God; it is not to alter, but to accomplish His counsels and bring us into the fruition of them. Thus, by these propositions, I have vindicated the unchangeableness of God from cavil and contradiction, and it remains a truth that the Lord Jehovah is an unchangeable God.

Chapter Six

*Several doctrinal corollaries or deductions from
the consideration of God's unchangeableness*

Having thus far asserted, opened, and vindicated
the unchangeableness of God, our next work shall
be to deduce some useful corollaries or conclusions
thence; and, indeed, many things of weight, and
things very momentous to us, may be drawn from
what has been said:

1. See here the glorious excellency and perfection of God, and that He is infinitely distinguished
from the creatures in dignity and glory. God is in
every way above and distinguished from the creatures. He is "the Excellent Glory" (2 Peter 1:17), and
there is hardly anything wherein His glorious excellency and perfection more brightly, illustriously,
and transcendently appear and shine forth than in
His unchangeableness. The creatures are all
changeable, one way or another; the heavens and
the earth, with all the furniture of the one and the
other, are changeable. "They shall perish, yea, all of
them shall wax old like a garment, and be changed
as a vesture" (Psalm 102:26). The day is coming
wherein "all these shall be dissolved" (2 Peter 3:11).
Men also are changeable; they indeed are changeableness itself, as it were. They are changeable in
their nature and changeable in their condition;

changeable in their spirits and changeable in their ways; changeable in their counsels and changeable in their comforts; changeable in all, they are "unstable as water," as it is said of Reuben (Genesis 49:4).

Great men are changeable (Psalm 62:9). Yes, good men are changeable; the best men are changeable; the best men at their best in this world are changeable, "Verily, every man at his best state is altogether vanity," that is, subject to change (Psalm 39:5). Men are not today what they were yesterday, nor will they be tomorrow what they are today; yes, men are today, and tomorrow they are not, so changeable are they. Yes, the angels, the blessed angels themselves are changeable. "God puts no trust in His saints, and His angels He charges with folly" (Job 4:18), that is, with possible, though not actual, folly; with change and folly in their nature, though not in their condition. There is a peccability in the very angels, I mean, in their nature. The best of creatures, in themselves, are subject to the worst of changes; the glorious angels are, in their nature, capable of sinning; indeed, in their condition they are not, being confirmed in both all holiness and all happiness by the grace of the second covenant, but in their nature they are. Hence that saying of one of the schoolmen, "Whatever creature there is that is impeccable, and cannot sin, he is not so from himself, or in his nature, but from the gift of free grace." Thus all creatures are changeable, but God is unchangeable. He is forever the same.

And oh, how glorious does this speak Him to be! And how does it distinguish Him from all the crea-

tures in perfection and glory! The truth is, this is a
glorious excellency and perfection in itself, and this
puts a luster and glory upon the excellencies and
perfections of God, for "this (as one speaks) is an attribute which, like the silken string through the
chain pearl, runs through all the rest and puts a
glory upon all." God's holiness would not be half so
glorious were it not unchangeable holiness. His
love would not be half so sweet were it not unchangeable love. His justice and wrath would not be
half so terrible were it not unchangeable justice and
wrath. Indeed, what would any of all His attributes
be in comparison were they not unchangeable? Oh,
let us learn to see and adore God in this glorious excellency and perfection of His.

2. From the consideration of God's unchangeableness, we conclude the transcendent excellency
of spiritual things beyond carnal, heavenly things
beyond earthly; and accordingly we should prize and
pursue the one and the other. Take this for an eternal rule: the nearer things come to God, and the
more they resemble Him and partake of Him, the
more excellent and desirable they are. Indeed, as
God is the fountain, so He is the measure and stan-
dard of all true worth and excellency. And there is
nothing that has any real worth or excellency in it
any further than it resembles Him and partakes of
Him. Now, what things most resemble God and partake of God? Are they spiritual or carnal, heavenly or
earthly? Surely they are spiritual and heavenly
things. God is unchangeable, and so in their kind
are these. As for carnal and earthly things, they are
fading and changeable; the best of them are

"treasures which moth and rust doth corrupt, and which thieves do break through and steal" (Matthew 6:19). They are all fading, dying, transient things. "The world passeth away" (1 John 2:17), that is, it is fleeting and perishing.

It is a good observation which Calvin had upon these words: "Because in the world there is nothing but what is fading and, as it were, but for a moment, the Apostle thence concludes how ill they consult and provide for themselves who carve out to themselves their happiness here, especially when God calls us to the blessed glory of eternal life. It is as if he should say, 'The true happiness which God offers to His children is eternal, and therefore most unworthy is it in us to encumber ourselves with this world, which, together with all its good things, will anon vanish away.' " Pray let us lay this observation to heart: "the world passes away," that is, riches, honors, and pleasures all fade and change and are short-lived. Alas! How soon, many times, riches change into poverty, pleasure into pain, honor into disgrace and contempt, friends into enemies, fullness into want! There is no stability in any of these things; they are subject to change every moment. But now spiritual and heavenly things are lasting and durable; they are "treasures which neither moth nor rust doth corrupt, nor can thieves break through and steal them" (Matthew 6:20). The riches of this world are uncertain riches, vanishing, disappearing riches (1 Timothy 6:17); but the riches of heaven and the covenant of God's love are certain, durable, and abiding riches.

Grace is a durable thing; the righteousness of

Christ is a durable, unchangeable thing; pardon, justification, acceptance with God through that righteousness are durable things; union and communion with God through Christ, these are unchangeable; these live and last forever where attained; and being so, they come nearer to God. They more resemble Him and partake of Him more than carnal and earthly things do, and so are more excellent than they, and should be accordingly prized by us.

O my beloved, there is more true worth and excellency in one dram of grace, one beam of holiness, one hint of pardon of sin, one sign of God's reconciled face, one embrace in the bosom of His love than there is in a world of carnal comforts and contentments. And accordingly we should prize and affect them. Our eye and heart should be taken off from the one and fixed upon the other. But alas! alas! We are apt to dote upon these changeable things here below. Oh, how fond are we of, and how passionately, for the most part, are we carried out after carnal, earthly, sensible things! But how cold are we in our love for, and pursuits after, things spiritual and heavenly! As if indeed earthly and not heavenly things were the only things of weight and moment, whereas indeed the one has no worth, no glory in it in comparison to the glory which exceeds. Let us therefore, with the holy Apostle, "look not at the things which are seen, but at the things which are not seen; for the things which are seen are temporal, but the things which are not seen are eternal" (2 Corinthians 4:18). Mark, the Apostle did not think carnal and earthly things worth a cast of his eye, because they are temporal, changeable; but spiritual things, which are durable and eternal, these he counted worthy of his eye and his heart and all. Oh, let us measure the worth of things by their resemblance to God, and what they partake of Him.

3. Behold here, as in a glass, the notorious folly and madness of such as prefer the creature before God in their choice and affections, placing their happiness in it and not in Him. Many (not one, or two, or a few, but many) say, "Who will show us any good?" And what good is it they would have shown them? Corn, wine, oil (Psalm 4:7)—creature-good, sensible-good, good to feed and fill a sensual appetite; and indeed, this is the good which most men prefer in their choice and affections before God, placing the rest and happiness of their souls therein. The generality of men have high thoughts of the creature and low thoughts of God, great affections for the creature and small affections for God. It is but here and there that one truly carries his happiness above the road of creatures and places it in God.

Take most men and it is the creature they love; it is the creature they prize; it is the creature they choose, and it is the creature they take up their rest and happiness in. As for God, they will have none of Him, as God complained of them of old: "Israel would none of Me" (Psalm 81:11). In a word, God and the creatures share the hearts and affections of the whole world between them. God offers Himself to men as the rest and happiness of their souls, and accordingly to be loved, to be prized, to be chosen, to be delighted in by them. On the other hand, the creatures offer themselves to men in like manner, and both plead for acceptance. And which, I pray, carries it, God or the creature? Truly the creature with most.

Alas! We are carnal, sensual, and naturally inclined to carnal and sensual things, embracing them to the neglect of God; and so the creature is preferred before God. Oh, what folly and madness is this! To prefer the creature before God in our choice and affections is not only to prefer emptiness before fullness, nothingness before sufficiency; but it is also to prefer vanity before immutability and variableness before unchangeableness. Oh, what folly, what madness is this! To prefer the creature before God in our choice and affections is to prefer a broken cistern that can hold no water before a fountain of living waters. So God Himself speaks of it, and withal brands it a black and horrid evil (Jeremiah 2:12–13), an evil which He calls upon the heavens to be astonished at and the earth to be horribly afraid of. O my beloved, to prefer a cistern before a fountain; a poor, narrow, scanty, borrowed good before a full, ample, original, all-sufficient good; a drop before an ocean of goodness and sweetness—this is great folly; but to prefer a broken cistern that can hold no water, before a fountain of living waters, fleeting nothingness before unchangeable fullness, this is greater folly, folly even to madness! And yet this is the folly of most men.

Carnal men are often in Scripture called "fools," and their folly appears in nothing more than their preferring changeable creatures before an unchangeable God. Indeed, than this what greater folly

can there be! We read of one who talked to his soul,
saying, "Soul, eat, drink, and be merry, for thou hast
much goods laid up for thee for many years; take
thine ease" (Luke 12:19). Mark it, he had never a
word of God in his mouth and (as we may safely
conclude) never a thought of God in his heart; but
he was wholly taken up with his barns, goods, and
treasures. And yet he bid his soul to take its ease, to
sit down at rest. God was as nothing with him and
the creature was all. Well, what title does Christ give
him? Does He give him the title of wise man? No,
"Thou fool." Christ called him a fool, as well He
might; for what greater folly is there than this, to be
wholly taken up with perishing creatures and neglect and forget an unchangeable God? Yes, and to
bid his soul take its ease too, because he abounded
with creature enjoyments. Indeed, had he said,
"Soul, take thine ease, be merry, thou hast heavenly
treasures laid up in abundance for thee; God is
yours, Christ is yours, the blessed Spirit, the
Comforter is yours, heaven, and eternal life are
yours," this would have been something suitable; but
to have his heart taken up with carnal things altogether, preferring them before God, and to bid his
soul to rest and be merry upon the account of these,
this is folly with a witness; and who does not deserve
the name of a fool if he does such? What shall I say?
This, namely to prefer the creature before God, is
such folly as will at last expose to shame and contempt forever all who are guilty of it, and such are
even hung up in chains for the highest instances of
folly and madness.

"Lo (says the psalmist), this is the man that made

not God his strength, but trusted in the abundance of his riches" (Psalm 52:7). Lo, this is the man who preferred the creature before God, who made riches, not God, his portion; this is that fool, that very fool, that madman, yes, and whoever they are who do this will at last (though, perhaps, too late) see and find themselves to be fools. "At his end (says the prophet concerning such a one) he shall be a fool" (Jeremiah 17:11). At his end he shall be a fool! What, was he a wise man in his beginning and progress? No, he was a fool all along; yet, though he was a fool, he thought himself wise. But at last he shall see his folly; he shall find that he was a very fool indeed, and, oh, how will the sight of such folly then vex and torment him! O sirs, when you shall see yourselves launching forth into an unchangeable state, as shortly you will, how will you then condemn yourselves of folly for preferring changeable creatures before an unchangeable God? Let me therefore speak to each of you, "Wilt thou set thine eyes upon that which is not? Riches make to themselves wings . . . cease from thine own wisdom, labor not to be rich" (Proverbs 23:4–5). Men think it to be their highest wisdom to get riches, but, sirs, know assuredly that this is folly. The only wisdom is to make sure of God, and get an interest in God; riches soon are not, but God always is, and He is the same forever.

4. From God's unchangeableness we infer the absolute necessity of a change in sinners if ever they are to be happy, if ever they are to be saved. My beloved, if ever sinners are saved and made eternally happy, there must be a change either in God or

them. Now in God there can be no change; the
change thereof must be in them. It is a rational and
undeniable way of arguing for a sinner to argue and
say, "God is unchangeable, and because God is unchangeable I must change or perish, change or die,
change or be miserable forever." For, pray, mark
that God never did and never will save any man in
his sins. He is, in Christ, infinitely willing, ready,
and able to save men *from* their sins. He sent and
sealed His Son on purpose to save men from their
sins, and accordingly gave Him a name suitable
hereunto, even Jesus, which signifies a Savior. "Thou
shalt call His name Jesus, for He shall save His people from their sins" (Matthew 1:21). But He never
did, and, unless He should change, He never will
save any *in* their sins. Without a change, therefore,
in us and upon us we are undone forever.

But a little further, yet to let you see the force of
this inference, and the rationality of such an argument, that it might fall with the greater weight and
conviction upon all our souls, be pleased to consider that it is utterly repugnant to, and inconsistent
with, the Word, nature, counsel, and oath of God to
save sinners without a change; for all these are absolutely and expressly against the happiness and salvation of unchanged souls, souls remaining still in
their sins, souls still in their natural state.

*The Word of God is against the happiness and salvation
of unchanged souls.* The Word of God says expressly
that without a change men may not, shall not, cannot be saved. The Word of God says, "The wicked
shall be turned into hell, and all that forget God"
(Psalm 9:17). The Word of God says that "into the

holy city there shall in no wise enter anything that defileth or worketh abomination" (Revelation 21: 27). The Word of God says that "the unrighteous shall not inherit the kingdom of God" (1 Corinthians 6:9). The Word of God says that "without holiness no man shall see God" (Hebrews 12:14). And lest all this should be thought to concern only profane and licentious ones, let me add that the Word of God says that "flesh and blood," that is, men in their natural state, "cannot inherit the kingdom of God" (1 Corinthians 15:50). Yes, the Word of God says, and that with an emphasis, that "except a man be born again," unless he is regenerated by the Spirit, "he cannot enter into the kingdom of heaven" (John 3:5). "Verily, verily (said Christ), except a man be born again," and again, "Verily, verily." He asserts it over and over, which notes, among other things, such as the weight of the truth asserted, our difficulty and adverseness to believe it and bow to it. Thus the Word of God is against this thing.

The nature of God is against the happiness and salvation of unchanged souls. The nature of God is infinitely pure and holy, and will not admit sinners to dwell with Him. "Thou art not a God that hath pleasure in wickedness, neither shall evil dwell with Thee" (Psalm 5:4). "The foolish (and such are all men by nature) shall not stand in Thy sight; Thou hateth all the workers of iniquity" (verse 5). "Thou art of purer eyes than to behold evil, and canst not look on iniquity" (Habakkuk 1:13), that is, without loathing and detestation. God's nature is holy, yes, it is holiness itself, and He can as soon cease to be God as cease to be holy. His nature is infinitely contrary to all sin, and He is infinitely contrary to all sin, and He infinitely, necessarily, and eternally hates all sin; sin, indeed, is strictly and properly the only object of God's hatred. His love is let out upon many objects, but sin is the only object of His hatred, and is not the nature of this God against the salvation of unchanged sinners? God must first cease to be infinitely holy, and so to be God, before sinners remaining in their unchanged state can be saved.

The counsel of God is against the salvation of unchanged souls. The law of the counsel of God is that we must be holy if ever we will be happy; that we must be called, justified, and sanctified if ever we would be glorified; so you find in that golden chain (as it is called): "Whom He did foreknow, He also did predestinate to be conformed unto the image of His Son. Moreover, whom He did predestinate, them He also called; and whom He called, them He also justified, and whom He justified, them He also glorified" (Romans 8:29–30).

The counsel, called here "the foreknowledge of God," tells us we must be changed, called, and justified if ever we are to be glorified. So expressly, "God hath chosen us to salvation" (2 Thessalonians 2:13). But how? Is there no need of a change? Yes, He has so chosen us as calls for a change: "He hath chosen us to salvation through the sanctification of the Spirit and belief of the truth." Yes, the counsel of God aims at holiness, and designs us primarily unto holiness. "He hath chosen us that we should be holy" (Ephesians 1:4). God must change all His counsels which have been of old, or sinners must be changed if ever they are to be saved.

The oath of God is against the salvation of unchanged sinners. God's oath is gone out of His mouth that no unbelieving, unchanged ones shall ever enter into His rest. "So I sware in My wrath, they shall not enter into My rest" (Hebrews 3:11).

Thus God's Word, His nature, His counsel, and His oath are all against the happiness and salvation of unchanged sinners; and God must change in all of those areas if ever they are to be saved without a change. But God can change in neither; the change must be in them. God being unchangeable, they must change or die, change or perish; and a double change must pass upon them or they cannot be saved—a change of their state and a change of their image: a change of their state in justification by the blood of Christ and a change of their image in regeneration and sanctification by the Spirit of Christ. Without both these they are undone forever.

(1) There must be a change of their state in justification through Christ's blood if ever they are to be saved. When a poor soul is "justified freely by grace, through the redemption that is in Jesus" (Romans 3:24), as the Apostle expresses it, when his sins are once pardoned and his person accepted with God by the imputation of Christ's perfect righteousness to him through believing, then is his state changed; and this change of state sinners must pass under, or, God being unchangeable, they cannot be saved. They must, through the blood and righteousness of Christ applied and appropriated in a way of believing, get their sins pardoned and their persons accepted. They must get all guilt removed and all

debts paid or they cannot possibly be saved. This is frequently mentioned in Scripture. "Being justified by faith, we have peace with God through our Lord Jesus Christ" (Romans 5:1). Again in verse 9: "Being justified through His blood, we shall be saved from wrath by Him." Again in verses 17–19: "If by one man's offense death reigned by one, much more they which receive abundance of grace and of the gift of righteousness shall reign in life by one, Jesus Christ. Therefore as by the offense of one judgment came upon all men to condemnation, so by the obedience of one shall many be made righteous." Still you see justification through the blood and righteousness of Christ is necessary unto life and salvation. "God hath made us accepted in the Beloved, in whom we have redemption through His blood, even the forgiveness of sins" (Ephesians 1: 6–7). The like is held forth in 1 Corinthians 6:11 and Romans 8:30. Oh, without pardon and justification through the blood of Christ there is no life, no salvation to be expected for sinners. Unpardoned sin will surely damn, and no pardon is to be had for sinners but in and by Christ, and union with Christ through believing. Once a soul is pardoned and justified by Christ through believing, then he has "passed from death to life" (John 5:24), but until that time he remains in death and under condemnation.

(2) There must be a change of their image in regeneration and sanctification by the Spirit of Christ. When a sinner is newly born, "born of water, and of the Spirit," as Christ's expression is, when he is made "a new creature, old things being passed away with him, and all things being become new"

(2 Corinthians 5:17), when he is "created in Jesus Christ" and has a sound work of grace wrought and carried on in him by the Spirit of Christ, then is his image changed; and such a change of image must sinners pass under or they cannot be saved. God never did and never will save an unrenewed soul. His unchangeableness will not admit the salvation of such a one; and indeed the Scripture is full in this regard. "Verily, verily (said Christ to Nicodemus), except a man be born again, he cannot see the kingdom of God" (John 3:3). And again in verse 5: "Verily, verily, except a man be born of water and of the Spirit, he cannot enter into the kingdom of God." You see that is what Christ asserts, and that over and over, and with the highest declarations imaginable. Hence also heaven is said to be the "inheritance of saints" (Colossians 1:12), and of "sanctified ones" (Acts 26:18). Hence the Corinthians are said to be "sanctified" as well as "justified," and so made capable of "inheriting the kingdom of God" (1 Corinthians 6:10–11). God is said, "according to His mercy," to save us "by the washing of regeneration, and the renewing of the Holy Ghost" (Titus 3:5). Thus a change of image as well as of state must pass upon us or we cannot be saved; and that because God is unchangeable. Oh, how should we all therefore look after this change!

Soul, assure yourself, it is not your civility and morality, however much raised and refined; it is not your external reformations; it is not your conforming yourself to the outward rules and laws of duty and the like that will save you, or avail you anything as to eternal life unless you come under this double

change of which you have heard. Paul, I am confi-
dent, could compare with you for morality and external conformity to the law when yet he was in a
lost state, and afterwards, coming to faith in Christ,
he saw cause "to account all but as lost and dung"
(Philippians 3:8). And he who came to Christ in
Matthew 19:16–22 had certainly attained to a great
degree of morality and external conformity to the
law, yet was lacking, and so far lacking that, for anything we find, he fell eternally short of heaven and
salvation. Oh, there must pass a change, a change of
state and a change of image, upon us or our morality will leave us at last to perish. Let us therefore
mind this change. Am I changed or not? Changed I
must be, and that with a great change, with a
change of state and a change of person, or I cannot
be saved. Have I therefore any acquaintance with
such a change? O my beloved, let unchangeableness
in God engage us all to look out after a change in
us; God will not change to save any of us all. He is
willing to change us that we may be saved, but He
Himself will not change to save any of us.

5. Again, from what has been declared touching
God's unchangeableness, we conclude and infer the
infinite sweetness of His love, the infinite bitterness
of His wrath, and so the exceeding happiness of
such as are interested in the one, and the extreme
misery of such as fall under the other. Sinners slight
God's love, preferring creature-love before it; and
they disregard His wrath, willfully provoking it
against themselves. But if they will view the one and
the other in the glass of His unchangeableness, they
will find that there is more sweetness in the one

than that it should be slighted, and more terribleness in the other than that it should be disregarded.

(1) From God's unchangeableness we conclude and infer the infinite sweetness of His love, and so the happiness of those who are interested in it. God has a people whom He loves, and His love for them is a free love, a rich love, a peculiar love, a love of singular eminence and perfection in all respects. But that which indeed crowns all and puts an infinite sweetness into it is this: it is an unchangeable love, a love that never fades, never varies. True, His love may be, and sometimes is, veiled and clouded; but though it is veiled it is not varied; though it is sometimes clouded, it is never changed. Love, under a veil or cloud, is still love. The sun may be under a cloud, yes, there may be an eclipse upon it for a time which may keep it out of our view and deprive us of the comfortable influences and shining of it for a season; but yet even then the sun is in being, and after a while it will shine again, and that as sweetly, brightly, and comfortably as ever. So there may be a veil, a cloud, an eclipse, as it were, upon God's love, such as may deprive us for a time of the comfortable views, shinings, and influences of it. But yet, even then it is love, and sweet love, too, and after a while it will shine and show itself again.

It is a sweet word which you have: "His anger endureth but a moment; in His favor is life. Weeping may endure for a night, but joy comes in the morning" (Psalm 30:5). Life here (as a judicious interpreter observed) is opposed to a moment, mentioned in the beginning of the verse; and so the sense is that that love wherewith God loves His people lasts throughout all life; it lives and lasts forever; it is a durable, abiding love. "In a little wrath I hid My face from thee, for a moment (says God to His Church); but with everlasting kindness will I have mercy on thee" (Isaiah 54:8). Thus, I say, though God's love toward His people may be veiled, yet it is never varied; it is a constant love, and oh, how sweet does this speak His love to be! And how happy are they who are interested in it! Oh, to be beloved by an unchangeable God with an unchangeable love, that is sweet indeed!

The creature's love has little worth or sweetness in it, and that not only because of its weakness and emptiness, but also because of its changeableness. Alas! The creature loves today and hates tomorrow. Oh, but now God's love is another manner of love, a love that has fullness and firmness, sufficiency and immutability both in it; and accordingly it must be infinitely sweet and desirable. Well therefore might David admiringly cry out as he did, "How excellent (or how precious) is Thy lovingkindness, O Lord?" (Psalm 36:7) and "Thy lovingkindness is better than life" (Psalm 63:3). It is before all loves; one dram of it is to be preferred before many worlds of creature enjoyments. God's love is all good, all comfort, all happiness in its fountain-fullness and purity; it is an eternal never-failing spring of sweetness, an invariable fountain of delight; in it there is grace, all grace; peace, all peace; joy, all joy; satisfaction, all satisfaction; rest and solace, all rest and solace. O soul, look upon the love of your God for you; look upon it and in it you will see unsearchable riches, unmeasurable fullness, unfathomable depths, and (which crowns all) eternal unchangeableness; and oh, how happy will you therein see yourself!

With what full consolation of spirit may you sit down and say, "God loves me, and He loves me unchangeably. Friends change, outward comforts change, I myself change; but God's love for me changes not. I am forever upon His heart. Nor can either men or devils, sins or sorrows cast me out of it. True, He sometimes afflicts me, but yet He loves me. He sometimes frowns upon me, but yet He loves me. He sometimes seems to slay me. He breaks me with breach upon breach, but yet He loves me. He confines me to a sick chamber. He lays me upon a sick bed. He seems to resolve to lay me in the dust, but yet He loves me; yes, all this is in love. I break with Him, and depart from Him, I am sinning against Him every day and hour; but yet He loves me. He loves me notwithstanding all. His love cannot be broken off from me, and after a while I shall bathe in the fountain thereof forever. Oh, sweet! Who would not long for this love? He loves me unchangeably, and He will therefore cleanse me, purify me, pardon me, make me perfectly holy. He loves me, and He will love me until He has lodged me in His own presence and bosom above, and there He will love me forever."

(2) From God's unchangeabless we conclude and infer the infinite bitterness of His wrath, and the extreme misery of all who fall under the weight thereof. God's love is not more sweet than His wrath is bitter. His love is not more desirable than His wrath is formidable, and that because He is an unchangeable God; and, oh, how miserable must they

be who fall under this wrath! We read of "the people of God's wrath" (Isaiah 10:6). There are some, then, who are properly "the people of God's wrath." They are children of wrath, heirs of wrath; and wrath, yes God's wrath, will be their portion forever; such are all finally impenitent and unbelieving ones, all who live and die in their impenitence and unbelief; and oh, how extremely miserable must they be! God's wrath is a great wrath, a fierce wrath, a sore wrath, a powerful wrath, an irresistible wrath, a burning, consuming, and devouring wrath, so Scripture speaks of it. All this speaks the exceeding bitterness and terribleness of it, and the extreme misery of such as fall under it; but that which adds even infinitely to all is that it is eternal and unchangeable wrath, wrath that abides forever. Hence it is set forth in Scripture by "unquenchable fire" (Matthew 3:12). God's wrath is called fire because of its exceeding heat and fierceness, being of a consuming and devouring nature, and it is called "unquenchable fire" because it is durable and unchangeable, it being what admits of no more change or period than His love does; and to fall under this unquenchable fire, under the revelation of this eternal, unchangeable wrath. Oh, how sad, how miserable must this be! Solomon tells us that "the wrath of a king is as the roaring of a lion" (Proverbs 19:12); and what, then, and how terrible, is the wrath of God, to whose wrath the wrath of all the kings on the earth is as nothing!

We are afraid sometimes of man's wrath, yes, so afraid of it as to suffer ourselves to be driven from our duty by it. But, my beloved, what is the wrath of man to the wrath of God? What is the wrath of a changeable man to the wrath of an unchangeable God? Let me say to each soul of you, as God by the prophet said to them, "Who art thou that thou shouldest be afraid of a man that shall die (a changeable creature), and forgettest the Lord thy maker?" (Isaiah 51:12–13). It is but a little while and man and his wrath both shall change and die, but God and His wrath will live forever. Oh, learn to fear and tremble at His wrath, and beware how for a little fading, changeable delight in sin you throw yourselves under unchangeable wrath and fury.

Poor sinner, you make light of God's wrath as if it were an inconsiderable thing; witness your willful and daily provoking of it against you by sin; witness your insensibleness of and under the tokens and revelations of it; witness your neglect of Christ, and of making your peace with God by Him, and the like. But soul, view it in the glass of His infinite unchangeableness and then see whether it is a thing to be made light of or not; the saints tremble just in the apprehension of it. "Who knows the power of Thine anger?" said Moses (Psalm 90:11). They sigh, they bleed, they groan, yes, they die, and are even distracted under a little temporal sprinklings and droppings of it (Psalm 88:15–16). Yes, they dread and tremble many times at but the revelation of it against others. "I was afraid (said Moses) of the anger and hot displeasure wherewith the Lord was wroth against you, to destroy you" (Deuteronomy 9:19). Moses could condemn the wrath of man, yes, of the man whose wrath of all men is most terrible, the wrath of a king (Hebrews 11:27); but yet he trembled at the wrath of God when it was provoked against others. Thus the saints tremble at God's wrath.

Yes, more, the devils themselves dread and tremble at God's wrath: "The devils believe and tremble" (James 2:19). They believe there is a God, and they tremble at the apprehension of the wrath of God. And sinner, whoever you are, however light you may now make of God's wrath, yet know that there is a time coming when you and the stoutest sinners in the world must and will tremble at it. See that one text: "The sinners in Zion are afraid; fearfulness hath surprised the hypocrites" (Isaiah 33:14). Why, what is the matter? Verily nothing but the sight and apprehension of God's wrath and vengeance coming upon them. So much do the following words in the same verse show: "Who among us shall dwell with devouring fire? Who among us shall dwell with everlasting burnings?" They saw God's wrath to be as a devouring fire; they saw the terror of it in the glass of God's unchangeableness, and therefore call it "everlasting burnings," and this filled them with dread and trembling.

Take one passage more: we find some "crying out to the mountains and rocks to fall on them, and hide them from the face of Him that sitteth upon the throne, and from the wrath of the Lamb; for (say they) the great day of His wrath is come, and who shall be able to stand?" (Revelation 6:16–17). Well, but who are they who thus cry out? Surely they are only a company of low-spirited creatures, you are thinking; they are only some women and children, or some base, cowardly ones who never had the spirit and courage of men. No, soul, they are no such persons; they are the kings of the earth, the great men, the rich men, the chief captains and mighty men, every bondman and every free man; all sorts of men, men of the highest place, the highest estates, the highest courage and valor, as well as others. These all are said to hide themselves in the dens and in the rocks of the mountains, and call unto the mountains and rocks, saying, "Fall on us."

The rocks reply, "Oh, but we will fall heavy."

"No matter, fall on us!"

"But to what purpose?"

"Why, to hide us from the wrath of God!"

"Time was you slighted and disregarded it as an inconsiderable thing; and do you so dread it now, and tremble at it now, that you cry to us rocks and mountains to fall on you, to hide you from it?"

"Oh, yes, good rocks, good mountains, fall on us. You will be light and easy upon us in comparison to what the wrath of God will do."

"How? Why should you think so? You had other thoughts of God's wrath a while ago; why do you so dread it and tremble at it now?"

"Oh, because 'the great day of His wrath is come, and none can stand before it.' We looked on this wrath a while ago at a distance, and then it seemed a light thing; but now 'the day,' yes, 'the great day of His wrath is come,' and there is no standing for us. While we looked at it at a distance, we could stand before it and make light of it; yes, in some lesser days of wrath we have borne up well enough, but now His wrath is come near us, yes, and the fullness and fierceness of it are breaking forth against us.

Now we see this wrath to be more dreadful and formidable, and that we can never stand up either under it or against it."

"So you do," reply the rocks and mountains, "then no wonder you cry to us to hide you from it; but truly 'tis more than we can do for you. You must now bear and grapple with that wrath forever, as to any relief we can afford you in the case."

O sinner! When the great day of God's wrath shall come, then, if not before, you also will tremble at His wrath. Indeed, now, would you see it and tremble at it, you might cry to a rock that could and would hide you from it, provided you get into it. I mean Christ, that Rock of Ages—He being embraced by faith, and your soul having union with Him—would hide and secure you against the wrath of God forever; but if you will go on to make light of this wrath, and to provoke it daily against you by sin, you will at last sink under the weight and burden thereof forever.

6. In the glass of God's unchangeableness we see the true reason why the best of us all are not consumed, and accordingly let us give the glory of it, where it is due. Beloved, why are you and I and others not consumed? True, we meet with some afflictions, and are exercised with some difficulties now and then, but why are we not utterly consumed and destroyed? Verily, it is not because we are able to save ourselves, nor is it because we deserve that God should save us, but it is purely and solely because our God is unchangeable. This account the text itself gives of it: "I am the Lord, I change not; therefore ye sons of Jacob are not consumed" (Malachi 3:6). All

our security lies in God's immutability: we perish not because He changes not. Pray give me leave a little to be free with you and myself. Why are we not consumed with an eternal consumption? We are sorely broken, many of us, it is true; we are broken in our estates, in our healths, in our comforts, in our relations, but why are we not utterly destroyed? Why are we alive? Why have we any one comfort about us? Yes more, why are we not consumed with an eternal consumption? Why are the best of us all not in hell? Why are we not stationed in an eternity of woe and misery? Why are we not now roaring and sweltering under the wrath of God? Why are we not companions with devils and damned spirits in everlasting burnings? Is it because our sins are few and small and have not deserved it? No, surely; why, then, is it? Because our God is unchangeable: unchangeable in being, counsel, covenant, and love. O my beloved! If we seriously consider what we are, and how we have carried it, what our sins and provocations have been, and how high they rise against the blessed God, and the like, we may well wonder we are out of hell, that we have a being anywhere on this side of the pit of perdition. Nor can we resolve it into any other cause but God's unchangeableness. Let me therefore entreat you to consider things a little, that you may give glory where it is due.

(1) Consider what you are, I mean, as to your nature and the depravity of it. You are a mere lump and mass of sin, enemies, yes, enmity itself against God and Christ (Romans 8:7). Your heart is a mere sink, a fountain, an abyss of sin and wickedness against God. "The heart is deceitful above all things,

and desperately wicked; who can know it?"
(Jeremiah 17:9). None but God can look to the bot-
tom of that sin, wickedness, and deceit that is in
your heart. Oh, the aboundings of sin that are found
in the best of us! Oh, the pride, the passion, the
earthliness, the sensuality, the uncleanness, the unbelief, the hypocrisy, the atheism, the disregard of
God, the aversion to all good, that dwells, works,
wars, and oftentimes prevails and predominates in
the hearts of the best saints, while here! Oh, the risings of sin and the aboundings of iniquity that are
found among us!

(2) Consider what you have done and how
you have carried it toward God. If you seriously consider things you will find, I fear, that you have done,
and to this day do, little else but sin against the
Lord. You have despised His goodness, abused His
love, violated His laws, trampled upon His authority,
grieved His Spirit, wounded His Son, darkened His
glory, and oftentimes struck even at His very crown
and being; yes, and "this has been your manner
from your youth" as God charged them of old
(Jeremiah 22:21). There is not that day, nor scarcely
that hour, wherein you have not sinned and do not
sin against God. Often have you made Him serve
with your sins, and wearied Him with your iniquities, as those of Isaiah 43:24. Your lives have been
lives of sin for the most part against God.

(3) Consider what black and horrid aggrava-
tion your sins are clothed with. Are not your sins, my
beloved, of a scarlet dye and crimson tincture? Are
they not heightened with many black and crying
aggravations? Have they not, at least many of them,

been committed against much love, much light, much mercy, many motions of the Spirit, many checks of conscience, many bonds and obligations to duty, many signal and eminent appearances of God to you, and for you; many tastes, many feelings of His love, and the like? What shall I say? Such in every way are our sins, yes, the sins of the best of us all that we cannot possibly look to the further end of them. "Who can understand his errors," said holy David in Psalm 19:12? David was a holy man, a man after God's own heart, and yet he cried out, "Who can understand his errors?" His sins were beyond search or understanding; and if his were so, what are ours? Truly, my beloved, our sins— in the number, nature, and aggravations of them— are beyond our reach, and well may we all with him cry out, "Who can understand his errors?"

(4) Consider what an infinite evil and demerit there is in every sin, even the least sin. As you are guilty of so much sin, and your sins are clothed, many of them, with so many and such crying aggravations, so you must know that there is evil enough in the least sin to damn you eternally, should God render the desert thereof to you. "The wages of sin is death" (Romans 6:23). Mark, the Apostle speaks of sin indefinitely, every sin, the least sin; and, said he, "the wages," that which is due to it, "is death." Every sin is an offense against God; it is infinitely contrary to His purity and holiness, His will and glory, His life and being. It is universally contrary to Him, and so much needs to have an inconceivable evil and demerit in it. "Every offense (said a learned man) against the chief good deserves the utmost punish-

ment, even the eternal destruction of the creature."
O sirs, we little think of the evil there is in a vain
thought, an idle word, an unholy, irregular action.
We little think of the evil the least sin carries in it.

(5) Consider how much God hates sin. Sin is
even infinitely odious and abominable to Him. "God
is of purer eyes than to behold iniquity" (Habakkuk
1:13), to wit, without loathing and detestation, and
He is once and again in Scripture represented as a
God who hates sin. Sin, indeed, is infinitely odious
in His sight.

Now let us weigh these things and lay them together, and then we shall see that it can be nothing
else that keeps us from destruction but God's unchangeableness, to which, therefore, we should give
the glory. It is the grace and love of God that first
bring us into a condition of life and salvation, and it
is the unchangeableness of God that keeps us there.
Truly, when some of us reflect a little upon ourselves, and consider what we are and have been in
our spirits and carriages toward God, how much we
have provoked Him, what frequent forfeitures we
have made and do make of our lives, souls, and all,
we see infinite cause to wonder that we are alive, that
the flames of divine wrath had not long since kin-
dled upon us, and the revenges of divine justice broken out against us. And blessed be God that we are
out of hell! Oh, that such a proud, such a stubborn,
such a stiff-necked people as we are should yet live!
That persons of so many and high provocations
against God as you, reader, and I are guilty of should
yet have a being out of hell! This is solely from the
unchangeableness of God. And, my beloved, we do

not rightly consider the matter if we do not see and acknowledge it to be so.

Oh, blessed be God for His unchangeableness! Had not God been unchangeable, where would I now be? I would now be shut up in the infernal pit. I would now be a companion with devils and damned spirits. I would now be separated from God forever; and how miserable then would I be! O my soul, adore the unchangeable One, and bless Him for His unchangeable counsel, His unchangeable covenant, His unchangeable love!

Chapter Seven

Several grounds of humbling from the consideration of God's unchangeableness, such as our unlikeness to Him therein, our charging Him with change, and our living so little upon His unchangeableness

As the unchangeableness of God is very teaching and instructive, so also very humbling, if rightly weighed and improved by us. There are several things which the consideration thereof calls aloud upon us to be humbled for, and, oh, that we would lay them to heart!

1. Is God unchangeable? Then how should we be humbled for our exceedingly great changeableness, and therein our unlikeness to God, the chief good! The more changeable we are in what is good, the more unlike God we are; and the more unlike God we are, the more cause we have of humbling. Oh, how should we loathe ourselves, and be abased at the foot of God in the sense of our great fickleness and changeableness! Alas! How changeable are we in all that is good! How changeable are many of us in our judgments and opinions, being "like children tossed to and fro, and carried about with every wind of doctrine" (Ephesians 4:14), being apt "to be soon removed from the faith of the gospel" (Galatians 1:6), as the Galatians were, at which Paul marvelled. How changeable are we in our affections

to God, and the things of God. Now the heart flames with love for God and Christ, and soon 'tis chilled and cold. Now we are full of holy longings and desires after God and Christ, grace and glory; we can say with the church of old, "The desire of our soul is unto Thee, O God, and to the remembrance of Thy name" (Isaiah 26:8). Yes, "Our soul thirsteth for God, for the living God; yea, as the hart panteth after the water brooks, so panteth our soul after God," as the psalmist speaks (Psalm 42:1–2). Soon there is not one holy breath to be found within us. No, we are even made up of worldly, sinful, unclean desires. "We pant after the dust of the earth" (Amos 2:7). We are thirsty for the creature, and nothing but that will satisfy us.

Now we delight in God and His ways. "We rejoice in the Lord, and our soul is joyful in our God," as it was with the church in Isaiah 61:10, and His ways are sweet and pleasant to us. His law is our delight. Soon we relish no sweetness; we take and exercise no joy, no delight, either in the one or in the other; but we drive on heavily, every duty being a burden to us, and the very thoughts of God a trouble.

Now we fear and stand in awe of God, not daring to sin against Him. We stand in awe of His presence; we stand in awe of His holiness; we stand in awe of His goodness; we stand in awe of His power, and the like. Soon we are fearless and regardless of Him, boldly venturing upon sinning against Him. Now we dread sin as hell itself, yea, and worse too; soon we embrace it and delight in it.

Again, how changeable are we in our holy purposes and resolutions! We take up this and that holy resolution; we purpose to walk so and so with God, to keep such and such a watch over our spirits and ways; to live more in communion with God, to drive a greater trade and design for heaven, and to hasten more to that better country, and the like. But, alas! How do such resolutions fade, change, and die within us! Few of them ever prove firm and effectual; yea, many times no sooner are such resolutions taken up by us but presently we run counter to them, and break with God more than before. The first temptation that comes turns us quite beside our purpose, and we miserably miscarry in the very things we resolved about. Our holy purposes are, for the most part, abortive. We turn aside "like a deceitful bow" as God complains of those in Psalm 78:57.

'Tis a sad complaint I have read in one of the ancients. "Oftentimes have I promised and resolved to amend, but I never made it good, but always I returned to sin and to my former wickedness. I added new and worse sins, and never reformed as I ought." And who of us may not, in a great measure, make the same complaint?

Yet, once more, how changeable are we in our ways and walkings! How uneven and inconstant in our goings! We have a heart that "loveth to wander" as God speaks of them of old in Jeremiah 14:10. Oh, the turnings aside, and, oh, the turnings back that we are guilty of in our walking with God! Oh, the gaps, pauses, and interruptions that are in our obedience! We should go on in one even, constant tenure of holy obedience; but, alas, we are in and out, off and on often within the day, yea, within the hour.

Yes, many times, sudden and great changes are found in our spirits and carriages toward God, and that for the worse. I'll give you but one instance of this, and that in an eminently holy man. This is an instance that may well make all of us tremble. "Sing unto the Lord, praise ye the Lord; for He hath delivered the soul of the poor from the hand of evildoers. Cursed be the day wherein I was born; let not the day wherein my mother bore me be blessed. Cursed be the man who brought tidings to my father, saying, 'A man-child is born unto thee,' making him very glad" (Jeremiah 20:13–15).

Pray mark, what a great change there was wrought in this good man's spirit, and that all of a sudden. In verse 13, he looks like one dropped out of heaven, and calling upon others so to do; but in verses 14 and 15, he looks rather like one broken loose out of hell, cursing himself and almost everyone about him. In the one he looks more like an angel than an imperfect saint; in the other he looks more like a devil than a man, so great was the change in his spirit, and this suddenly made. After he had, in verse 13, been praising God, and was, as it were, taken up to heaven, the very next news you hear of him is that he is full of cursing. And truly just as changeable are we *all* here. Oh, how suddenly, many times, do we change and fall from the best into the worst of frames and carriages before God— from love to hatred; from faith to unbelief; from holy fear to carnal security; from obedience to rebellion; from delight in God to a neglect of God, and a weariness of His ways and presence. Oh, let us be humbled for our exceeding changeableness, and therein our unlikeness to God in His unchangeableness.

2. Is God unchangeable? Then how should we be humbled that we so often wrong God, charging Him with inconstancy and change as we do! Such, my beloved, is the enmity and unbelief of our hearts that we are apt, upon all occasions, to take up hard thoughts of God and bring in black charges against Him. Now we charge Him with weakness, and soon with folly; now with unfaithfulness, and soon with injustice; now with cruelty, and soon with change; which is the great evil, and calls for great humbling. God is unchangeable, and He stands much upon the glory of His unchangeableness; and yet we charge Him with change. What an affront is this! This the psalmist, whoever he was, came near unto. "Will the Lord cast off forever? And will He be favorable no more? Is His mercy clean gone forever? Doth His promise fail for evermore? Hath God forgotten to be gracious? Hath He in anger shut up His tender mercies?" (Psalm 77:7–9). What is all this but in effect a charging of God with change?

He is here even upon the point of concluding that God is not the God He was, that He is not so merciful nor so faithful nor so gracious as formerly He was. It is as if He should have said, "God was a God of mercy. Mercy pleased Him, but now His mercy is at an end, and He has become all severity; He was faithful in His promises, but now His promises fail, and fail utterly. He was a gracious God. Grace was His darling attribute, but now His grace is forgotten by Him."

Thus for a time He charged God with change,

though afterwards, as the context tells us, his faith recovered itself and he came to right thoughts of God again. Job also was deeply involved with his guilt. "Thou art turned to be cruel to me," said he to God in Job 30:21. "Thou wert a kind God, but now Thou art a cruel God to me."

The church also is full of this, as Isaiah speaks out: "Zion said, 'The Lord hath forsaken me, and my God hath forgotten me' " (Isaiah 49:14). This is to say, "God has changed. He is not the God He was."

Thus I say, though God is unchangeable, yet we are apt to charge Him with change. We are apt to think that He is neither *what* He was nor *where* He was; that He is either not as good as He was, or else not so great, so powerful, so wise, so holy, so faithful, so gracious as He was, and the like. "Behold (said the prophet), the Lord's hand is not shortened, that it cannot save; neither is His ear heavy, that it cannot hear" (Isaiah 59:1). They thought and concluded that God's hand was shortened, that is, that His power was lessened, and that He was not as able to save now as formerly. They thought and concluded that His ear was grown heavy, that is, that He was not as good and kind and ready to hear their prayers now as formerly. He was a God able to save, but now, say they, He is not. He was a prayer-hearing God, but now, say they, He is not. Thus they were ready to charge Him with change. But, said the prophet, there is no such matter. God is what He was. His power is the same, and His readiness to hear, help, and save is the same as ever it was.

There are, among others, two cases especially in which we are apt to charge the unchangeable God

with change. One is when we change in our carriages and behavior towards God; the other is when
God's carriages and dispensations are changed towards us; for indeed we are apt to measure God and
judge Him by His outward carriage and dispensations towards us. And when they are changed, we
conclude He is changed.

"And Jacob beheld the countenance of Laban,
and behold, it was not toward him as before"
(Genesis 31:2). So we, many times, behold the countenance of God, His outward carriage and dispensation toward us, and 'tis not towards us as before. His
countenance is changed; and because His countenance is not the same, we think His heart is not toward us as formerly, but has changed. O my beloved,
let us take heed of this grand evil of charging God
with change; 'tis indeed a grand evil, 'tis very
grievous and provoking to God, and 'tis what lays
the soul under much deep-dyed guilt; 'tis indeed to
rob God of one of the brightest jewels in His crown.
Yes, 'tis to un-God Him; for if He is changeable, He
is not God. Tremble, therefore, reader, and tremble,
O my soul, at the thoughts of such a thing as this: to
charge the unchangeable One with change.

3. Is God unchangeable? Then how should we be
humbled that we live so much upon the creature,
and so little upon God; so much upon the creature
that does change, and so little upon God who
changes not! If we reflect seriously upon ourselves,
we shall find (at least many of us) that we live more
upon the creatures than we do upon God; more
upon broken cisterns than upon this fountain of living waters. The best and holiest of us will find that

we live too much upon the creature and too little upon God.

Witness the eagerness, strength, and vehemence of our desires after the creature more than after God and communion with Him. Alas, how passionately, many times, do we long, and how vigorously do we pursue after the creature when we can be content well enough without God and communion with God! Witness the frequency of our thoughts and contemplations of and about the creature more than of God and about God. Alas! As those did, "We mind earthly things" (Philippians 3:19), but how seldom do we think of God and contemplate Him!

Now that which is most in our thoughts is that which we live most upon; witness our delight and complacency in the creature more than in God. Oh, what fresh, springing, vigorous delights have we many times in the creature! But when and how little do we delight ourselves in God!

Now that which we take most delight and complacency in is that we live most upon. Witness our immoderate griefs, and the bitterness of spirit we are usually in over the loss or withdrawal of the creatures more than over the loss and withdrawal of God and His presence from us. Let this or the other creature comfort be withdrawn from us, and how do we take on usually! And what bitterness of soul are we filled with! Then with Hagar we "lift up our voice and weep" (Genesis 21:16). How did Jonah, that good man, take on when the gourd was withered (Jonah 4:7–9). But how seldom do we grieve, bleed, and mourn for want of communion with God! Yes, how indifferent, for the most part, are we whether we have communion with God or not! And what does this argue but that we live too much upon the creature and too little upon God?

Thus, if we seriously reflect upon ourselves, we shall find, by these and such like things as these, that we live more upon the creatures than we do upon God. Oh, how humbling should this be upon us! The creatures are vain, fading, changeable things. They are even vanity and changeableness itself; but God is an eternal, unchangeable good. He is the same forever, an unchangeable fountain of all goodness, sweetness, blessedness, and delight.

Now to live upon these changeable creatures, and not upon this unchangeable God, is a great evil, and calls for great mourning and humbling at our hands. 'Tis a great speech I have read in Augustine, wherein he bewails this very sin: "He that made me is good, and He is my good; but in this I sinned that not in Him, but in His creatures, I sought myself, and my other pleasures." That is, I took up my solace and happiness in the creatures, and not in God. And what then? "And so I ran myself upon many sufferings, errors, and confusion of soul."

And may not many of us make the very same complaint? We live upon changeable creatures more than upon an unchangeable God; and hereby God is dishonored, His Spirit is grieved, and our souls are bereaved of good, yes, the best good, the good of grace, and divine discoveries and communications. Hereby we eat husks when we might eat bread; and we drink garbage when we might drink wine in our Father's house. Hereby we are exposed to sorrows, snares, and death, yes, and hereby we are in danger of being excluded from God forever.

O my beloved, let us be convinced of this evil, and mourn over it! For my own part, when I reflect upon myself, I find cause to fear that I have lived upon creatures all my days, upon changeable creatures, to the great, if not total, neglect of the unchangeable God; and believe it, 'tis a hard thing to come off from the one to live so purely and entirely upon the other as we ought to do. May the Lord humble us for these things.

Chapter Eight

God has a revenue of honor due to Him upon the account of His unchangeableness. We should give Him that honor. Several short and plain directions in order thereto

Every attribute or perfection of God has a revenue of honor and glory due to it from the creature; and 'tis a great part of both the wisdom and duty of the creature to give to each attribute and perfection of His its proper glory. God is pleased to reveal and discover Himself, sometimes in one and sometimes in another attribute of His. Sometimes He reveals Himself in His wisdom, sometimes in His faithfulness, sometimes in His justice, sometimes in His grace, sometimes in His greatness, and sometimes, as here, in His unchangeableness. Now, I say, a great part of a Christian's skill and duty lies in this, to give to each attribute in which God reveals Himself its proper glory; that is to say, to honor God suitably to the present revelation He makes of Himself. Now, God being unchangeable, our work and care should be to give Him the glory of His unchangeableness, which, let me tell you, is very dear to Him.

But how may we give God the glory due to this attribute of His? Take only these few plain directions as to that briefly.

1. Would we give God the glory of His unchange-

ableness? Then let us get our hearts deeply affected with this attribute of His, being in a holy manner overawed therewith. The unchangeableness of God is an attribute that demands much holy awe and dread from the creature; and when our hearts are indeed in a holy manner overawed with the sense of this attribute and we are filled with a reverential regard of God, as He is an unchangeable God, then do we give Him the glory thereof. This seems to be pointed at in Isaiah. God reveals Himself in His unchangeableness when He says, "I, the Lord, the first and the last; I am the first, and the last" (Isaiah 41: 4–5), or, as some render it, "I the same, I the same." In verse 5 you have the isles affected and overawed with this attribute: "The isles saw it and feared."

Accordingly, if we would indeed give God the glory of His unchangeableness, we should labor to get our hearts overawed with the sense and apprehension thereof; we should dwell much in meditation on this perfection of God. Our language should be, "Well, however changeable we are, yet God is unchangeable. He is forever the same, unchangeable in greatness, unchangeable in goodness, unchangeable in wisdom, unchangeable in power, unchangeable in holiness, unchangeable in faithfulness, unchangeable in fullness and sufficiency. He is in every way an unchangeable God. What He was, He is; what He is, He will be forever." Thus we should sit down and contemplate this attribute until we find our hearts affected and overawed by it.

2. Would we give God the glory of His unchangeableness? Then let us ascribe this attribute to God, and celebrate His glory in it. In Deuteronomy 32:3,

we are called upon to "ascribe greatness to God," and, as we should ascribe greatness, so we must ascribe unchangeableness to God, and withal admire and adore Him therein if we mean to give Him the glory of this attribute of His. This the psalmist does once and again. "From everlasting to everlasting, Thou art God" (Psalm 90:2). And again, "They shall perish (speaking of the heavens), but Thou, Lord, shalt endure; they shall be changed, but Thou art the same, and Thy years shall have no end" (Psalm 102:26–27). He celebrates the glory of God in His unchangeableness, admiring and adoring Him in this perfection of His.

The church does the same thing, where we read of "four beasts which rest not day and night, saying, 'Holy, holy, holy, Lord God Almighty, which was, and is, and is to come' " (Revelation 4:8). Mark, first, they celebrate the glory of God's holiness, saying, "Holy, holy, holy." Second, they celebrate the glory of God's power and sovereignty: "Lord God Almighty." Third, they celebrate the glory of God's unchangeableness and eternity, "which was, which is, and which is to come." In other words, "Thou art a holy God, and we adore Thee for Thy holiness; Thou are a potent and sovereign Lord, and we adore Thee for Thy power and sovereignty; Thou art an unchangeable God, and we adore Thee for Thy unchangeableness. However fading the creatures are, Thou art still the same."

In like manner should we do. We should ascribe unchangeableness to God, and be much in admiring and adoring Him for and in this perfection of His. This is all that we can do, and 'tis indeed our glorifying of Him to display and make mention of the excellencies and perfections of God, and with both our spirits and tongues to celebrate the glory of them, which indeed will be our work forever. Oh, let us be much in it now!

3. Would we give God the glory of His unchangeableness? Then let us see and acknowledge Him and His unchangeableness to be the sole spring and fountain of all that unchangeableness that either men or angels attain unto. The creatures—men and angels not excepted—in themselves are all changeable, but there is a blessed unchangeableness which some of them, I mean, the saints and holy angels, at last attain unto. They are (as the schoolmen speak of them) eternally and unchangeably confirmed in all good, in all holiness, all happiness. And whence comes this to pass? Verily, from the unchangeableness of God, that is the spring and fountain of all. Were not God unchangeable, unchangeable in His covenant, counsel, and love, they would never arrive at such an unchangeableness; to God's unchangeableness therefore we should give the glory of it.

As Christ said in another case, "Because I live, ye shall live also" (John 14:19). So may God say, both to men and angels, "Because I am unchangeable, therefore shall you be unchangeable also." Indeed, the unchangeableness which saints and angels attain unto is but a beam, as it were, of God's unchangeableness, emitted down upon them; they shall be unchangeably holy because God is so; they are unchangeably blessed because God is so; and they have communion with Him by Christ in His unchangeable holiness and blessedness. See, there-

fore, and acknowledge God and His unchangeableness in that unchangeableness which saints and
angels attain unto, ascribing theirs wholly to His.

4. Would we give God the glory of His unchangeableness? Then let us live upon this unchangeableness of His. The more we live upon the unchangeableness of God, the more we honor it and give Him
the glory of it. Now we should live upon it under a
double notion.

First, we should live upon it as the sole cause of
all our preservation, expecting all from it and ascribing all to it. This God required from us in our very
text: "I am the Lord, I change not, therefore ye are
not consumed." In other words, "'Tis from My unchangeableness that you are alive, that you are out of
hell, and 'tis My unchangeableness that must keep
you alive, and preserve you forever, and I expect you
should own it and live upon it accordingly."

Our language should be, "I am alive, and why?
Because God is unchangeable. Yes, I hope I shall
live, and that forever; but why? Because God is unchangeable. True, I am a changeable creature, and,
being left to myself, I shall quickly forfeit life, soul,
salvation, and all. Yes, I am forfeiting all every day
and hour by sin; but God is an unchangeable God.
He is forever the same. His counsel, His covenant,
His love are all unchangeable, and therefore I live,
and shall live, yes, live eternally."

Oh, this is so to live upon the unchangeableness
of God as to give Him the glory of that perfection of
His!

Second, we should live upon the unchangeableness of God as a sweet spring of comfort and re-

freshment to us under the many afflictive changes, which here in this world we meet with. Changes and war are upon us, but the unchangeableness of God is a sweet spring of comfort and refreshment in all and under all. And when we live upon it as such, bearing up our souls thereupon, then do we give this attribute its proper glory. This is what is called for: "Trust ye in the Lord forever." That is, live, rest, depend upon Him. Why so? "For in the Lord Jehovah is everlasting strength" (Isaiah 26:4). The words could be translated as "the rock of ages," "the rock of this age," "the rock of former ages," "the rock of ages to come," "a rock of all ages," and "the rock of all ages." That is to say, God is a firm, un-changeable One; and, being such a One, He is and must be the proper object of trust, and unless we trust in Him and live upon Him as our life, we do not give Him His proper glory.

We should say, "Though my estate changes, yet God does not change, and so long all is well. Though my friends and comforts change, my friends turn enemies, and my comforts become crosses, yet God does not change, and so long all is well. Yes, 'tis true, my spirit changes; there is no fixedness, no stability in it, as to anything that is good and gracious. Yet, however, God changes not. He is always the same, and I'll live on Him."

"The Lord lives, and blessed be my Rock," said David in Psalm 18:46. Friends die, trade dies, and I myself am dying, but the Lord lives; and there is enough in that to bear me up under all. Oh, when thus we live upon God's unchangeableness as a spring and fountain of comfort to us under all afflictive changes here, then do we give Him the glory of this attribute of His.

5. Would we give God the glory of His unchangeableness? Then let us labor to imitate Him, and to be like Him herein as much as we possibly can. Let us labor, as much as possible, for a holy unchangeableness, a fixedness and stability in what is good, even here, and that in conformity to God. We cast an honor (as one observed) upon those whom we imitate; for by our imitation of them we acknowledge an excellency in them, which is all that honoring in the first notion of it imports. Sure I am, the more like God we covet to be, and the more we imitate Him in this perfection of His by coming up to a holy evenness and stability in what is good, the more we honor Him and give Him His proper glory. But this may possibly be addressed as a chapter by itself in its proper place. Thus you see how to give God that glory which is due to Him upon the account of His unchangeableness.

Chapter Nine

God's unchangeableness should induce us to choose Him for our God and portion, and to take up the rest and happiness of our souls in Him, with arguments to quicken thereunto

The unchangeableness of God calls aloud upon us all to choose Him for our God and portion, and to take up the rest and happiness of our souls in Him and not in the creatures. The truth is, to choose God for our God and portion, and to take up our rest and happiness in Him, is what every discovery of God, in one or another excellency or perfection of His, requires and calls for at our hands. Does He reveal Himself to be a holy God? This calls upon us to choose Him for our God and portion, and to get an interest in His holiness. Does God reveal Himself to be a gracious God, a God of grace and love? This calls upon us to choose Him for our God and portion, and to get an interest in His love. Does He reveal Himself to be a faithful God, a God who keeps covenant and mercy? This calls upon us to choose Him for our God and portion, and to get an interest in His faithfulness.

So here, does God reveal Himself to be an unchangeable God? This calls upon us to choose Him for our God and portion, and to get an interest in His unchangeableness, taking up the rest and happiness of our souls in Him, and, accordingly, oh, that we would look and live above changeable creatures, taking up our rest and happiness in this unchangeable God, which to do is infinitely our safest and sweetest course. For pray consider, who or what will you choose for your portion, and wherein will you place the rest and happiness of your souls if not in the unchangeable God? Sure I am, you have but God or the creature to make choice of; now what is the creature to God? What is the changeable creature to an unchangeable God? Alas! The one is infinitely short of the other. God indeed is in every way, and in all respects, a most desirable good. He is an original good, a full good, a suitable good, a satisfying good, an unmixed good, an all-sufficient good, and, which crowns all, an unchangeable good, a good that never fades, never fails. "He is the living God, and steadfast forever" (Daniel 6:26). The creatures are all changeable and perishing. A heathen could say, "We live among perishing things." And it was a great saying of one of the ancients, "We have nothing here of any long continuance; and all the felicity of this world is gone while we hold it, and lost even while we enjoy it." So great is the changeableness and uncertainty of all these things.

But God, as you have heard, and all that good that is in Him, is always and forever the same, which speaks Him to be infinitely sweet and desirable, and so infinitely worthy to be embraced by us for our God and portion. This indeed crowns and perfects all that good that is in God. Look, as the changeableness of the creatures lowers and contaminates all that good and sweetness that are in them, so the

unchangeableness of God infinitely raises and com-
mends that good and excellency that are in Him.
Had the creatures ten thousand times more good
and excellency in them than they have, yet this one
consideration that they are changeable would be
enough to damp and quash all. Though the creatures had never so much sweetness and goodness in
them, and though I had never so full, free and ample enjoyment of them; though the streams ran
never so pleasantly on each hand of me, yet this one
thought, that all this is fading and changeable and
will last but for a season, would be enough to alloy
my joy and even embitter all to me. So, on the other
hand, though God is such an infinite ocean of
goodness, sweetness, and blessedness as He is, yet
that which crowns all is His unchangeableness in
all; without this, the whole of God could not make
us happy.

Now, shall the consideration hereof induce you
to choose Him for your God and portion, and take
up your rest and happiness in Him forever? Possibly
you have never yet chosen God to be your God and
portion, nor have you taken up the rest and happiness of your souls in Him. You have chosen the creatures; you have chosen this world; you have chosen
carnal, sensual things, and in these have you placed
your rest and happiness. But, as for God, He has
hitherto been distant from your thoughts; you have
centered in changeable creatures and forgotten the
unchangeable God. But will you now change your
choice and take up a new rest? Oh, now let an unchangeable God—not changeable creatures—be
your God and portion, your rest and happiness. Oh,

that the language of your souls to God might now be
that of the psalmist: "Whom have I in heaven but
Thee? And there is none upon earth that I desire besides Thee" (Psalm 73:25). "Lord, Thou, and Thou
alone, shall be my God, my rest, my portion, my
happiness, and my all forever. Indeed, I had chosen
the creatures for my portion and happiness, but now
I renounce that choice. I will have no more to do
with changeable creatures. The world was my happiness, and I sat down with it, so foolish was I and
ignorant; but now I have done with the world—this
fleeting, fading, dying world—and Thou, Lord,
alone shall be my all forever."

Oh, that you would indeed thus choose the unchangeable God, and take up your rest and happiness in Him this day! And you who have chosen
Him, and taken up your happiness in Him, make a
new choice of Him, and take up your rest more
purely and entirely in Him. Say of this unchangeable One, "This God is our God forever and ever"
(Psalm 48:14). Oh, labor to get more above the creatures, and live more in God, and upon God. The
more purely and entirely you take up your rest in
God, the sweeter will He be to you, and the more satisfaction will your souls find in Him. Now to
quicken you thus to choose God, and to live upon
Him and His unchangeableness:

1. Consider what a changeable world we live in.
We live in a changeable world, in a world that
brings many great changes every day. The truth is,
this world is a very changeable world, and it is not
long before it will be changed once for all. The day
is coming when "all these things shall be dissolved;

the heavens shall pass away with a noise, and the
earth shall melt with fervent heat" (2 Peter 3:10). In
the meantime, the world is not without its changes;
and how great changes we may live to see, who
knows? Such changes seem to be coming upon the
world that nothing but an unchangeable God will
be able to bear us up under them. We read of "distress of nations which shall be upon the earth, with
perplexity; men's hearts failing them for fear, and
for looking after those things that shall come to
pass upon the earth" (Luke 21:25–26). The sum
amounts to this: there shall be such changes, such
rendings, such shakings, such terrible convulsions
and concussions wrought in the nations of the
world; such desolations shall be made, and such terrible storms of wrath and vengeance shall fall upon
the world, that men shall be even made lifeless with
fear and driven to their wits' end. They shall fall under a swooning of spirit; they shall breathe out their
very souls, or they shall be filled with such anguish,
horror, and confusion of soul that they shall be
ready to lay violent hands upon themselves and take
away their own lives. And, my beloved, should we live
to see such things, how good will an unchangeable
God be! O sirs! Living in such a changeable world,
who would not fix upon an unchangeable God as a
man's portion and happiness? Who would not get
upon, yes, *into* this Rock of Ages? And how good,
how sweet will it be to have an unchangeable God to
retreat to, and take refuge in!

2. Consider what changeable things all our creature comforts and contentments are. As the world
wherein we live is a changeable world, so all our

creature comforts are changeable comforts. Should the world stand where it does and as it does, without any such changes as we have mentioned, yet our best creature comforts here are subject to change every day. And how soon we may say of one or another or all of them, as Jacob sometimes did of his two sons, Joseph and Simeon, "Joseph is not, and Simeon is not" (Genesis 42:36)? How soon we may say, "This and that comfort are not. Who can tell? I have now a trade; tomorrow, it may be, I shall have none. I have now an estate; tomorrow, it may be, I shall have none. I have now a pleasant habitation; tomorrow, it may be, it will be in ashes. I have now my friends and relations about me, my husband, or my wife lying pleasantly in my bosom, my children like olive branches round about my table; tomorrow, it may be, they will all sleep in the dust and go down to the gates of the grave, and I shall see them no more."

Alas! These things are not (as Solomon speaks of riches); such is their changeableness that they scarcely have a being; or, suppose these things should stay with us, yet how soon may they be embittered to us? How soon may the best of this wine be turned into wormwood? How soon may the sweetness of these comforts be changed into bitter crosses? Sometimes the desire of our eyes is taken away from us with a stroke (as God threatened Job of old), that is, suddenly; and whenever we are aware of it our dearest, sweetest, and most delightful comforts are taken from us. At other times the desire of our eyes becomes the burden of our souls; our dearest comforts are embittered to us; that which yesterday was sweet and pleasant, today, possibly, is bitter and burdensome to us; that which today is the joy of our hearts, tomorrow it may well be as a goad in our sides, and as thorns in our eyes. Oh, how soon, many times, do our most pleasant streams turn into waters of Marah to us! Now all on this side, God being thus changeable, who would not rest in Him and His unchangeableness? O unchangeableness! Unchangeableness! This is to be found in God alone, and therefore let Him alone be the rest and portion of our souls.

3. Consider how near our last and great change is unto us. Should the world never become old, nor admit of any change; and should our creature comforts and contentments live and last forever, yet we ourselves must change. We are fading, dying, perishing creatures; we pass under many changes, and great changes, and it is but a little while before our last and great change will come. Death is our last and great change until the resurrection. So the Holy Ghost by Job speaks of it in Job 14:14, and this is a great change indeed, a change from work toward reward, from time to eternity; a change out of this world into another; from these tabernacles of clay to live in eternal regions, either of light or darkness; and thus shall we all be changed. A few years, a few months, a few weeks, a few days, a few hours, yes, it may be, just a few moments more and we shall all be thus changed, changed by death out of time into eternity, and how much then should we be concerned to make choice of, and take up our rest in, an unchangeable God! Then, namely when we pass under this change, to be sure nothing but unchangeableness will be of any avail to us, and this is

to be found in God alone; Him therefore should we choose, and take up our rest in.

This very condition induced David to make a fresh choice of God, and cleave more entirely to Him, as his rest and happiness. "Behold, O Lord, Thou hast made my days as a hand-breadth, and mine age is as nothing before Thee. Verily, every man at his best state is altogether vanity; surely every man walketh in a vain show; surely they are disquieted in vain" (Psalm 39:5–6). Well, and what now? Why, says he, "And now, Lord, what wait I for? My hope is in Thee" (verse 7). He saw his vanity and changeableness, as also the vanity and changeableness of all others, both persons and things; he saw both himself and all others in their very best state to be not only vain, but even vanity itself, subject to change every hour; in the light and sense of which he cleaves to God, chooses Him, centers in Him as his God, his portion, his all.

"Now Lord what wait I for? My hope is in Thee." Now, Lord, that I have seen my own vanity and changeableness, and the vanity and changeableness of others too, now I look to You, I cleave to You, I rest in You as my only good, portion, and happiness. I have now done with the streams, with the creatures, and with creature contentments, and I will now bathe only in the fountain, rest wholly in Yourself, the fountain of living waters. And, my beloved, did we dwell more in the consideration of the nearness of our last and great change, we should doubtless cleave more closely and entirely to the unchangeable God, as our rest and portion. Our thus numbering our days, with deep and frequent con-

sideration of the shortness of our lives, and how
soon we may be changed, would make us apply our
hearts to this wisdom (Psalm 90:12), to get an interest in the unchangeable God. Oh, be much therefore in this work!

4. Consider that then, and not until then, shall
we be happy indeed, when we come to look and live
above changeable creatures upon an unchangeable
God. It is happiness, my beloved, that is the great interest of souls, and it is happiness we all desire or
pursue after; now then are we happy indeed, and not
until then, when we get above the creatures, and
take up our rest in the unchangeable God. Pray, sirs,
let us consider things a little; suppose you had this
whole world at will, and might enjoy as much of the
creature as your souls could wish; suppose you could
live all your days in a paradise of all earthly delights,
and swim chin-deep in the streams of all creature-
contentments; yet what were all this? Alas! It would
not make up one dram of true happiness; your happiness must be in God still. Mind how the psalmist
speaks to this: "Happy is the people that is in such a
case; yea, happy is that people whose God is the
Lord" (Psalm 144:15). In what case was this? Why, a
case of outward prosperity, a case of enjoying an affluence of all outward creature contentments; for of
these he had spoken before. But "David, is this really
your judgment, and do you give it us for a divine
truth, that these things make men happy?" "No (says
he), I rather herein tell you what the world's judgment is, and wherein they look upon happiness to
consist." They think those of all others to be the
happiest people who enjoy most of this world, most

ease, most pleasure, most of creature comforts. But
(says he), "I am of another mind. I account them the
happy people who have the Lord for their God, that
is, who have a covenant relation to and interest in
the blessed God." It is God, not the creature, the enjoyment of whom makes happy.

The former proposition ("Happy is the people
that is in such a case") shows what carnal men judge
concerning happiness, and what makes happy in
their account; the latter proposition, "Happy is the
people whose God is the Lord," shows what true
happiness indeed is and wherein it consists, which
is in an interest in God, in the unchangeable One.
Or, "This latter is (as one observes) a correction of
the former, and it is as if he should say, 'They are
the happy souls, who have the true God, not the
changeable creature, propitious to them.' " Oh, it is
not the creature, but God, and interest in and communion with unchangeableness, that makes happy.
It is the joint language of all the creatures:
"Happiness is not in us; we are all vanity, and subject
to change, and cannot make eternal souls happy."
Happiness lies in God alone, where alone both fullness and unchangeableness, sufficiency and immutability are to be found. To look for happiness in
the creature is to seek the living among the dead;
but to look for it in God is to seek it at the fountainhead of all true happiness.

What shall I say? God is His own happiness. He is
eternally blessed in and with Himself, (as has been
before declared), and He is the happiness of His
creatures, both saints and angels; and when God
makes His people, His saints and servants, perfectly

happy, which He never does until He takes them to heaven, He then takes them from all their creature contentments, and He admits and receives them into the full and single enjoyment of Himself.

It would be easy to show that nothing short of God and His unchangeableness can possibly make us happy, and accordingly we shall never be happy indeed until we learn to carry our happiness above the road of creatures, and place it wholly and entirely in God. But I must not run out too far here. O my beloved, that man is certainly happiest whose heart and life are holiest, and whose communion with God is fullest; he who enjoys most of God, whether he enjoys much or little of the creature, he it is that is most happy. It is a great saying which I have read in Augustine, speaking to those who seek happiness in the creature: "Seek what you seek, that is, seek happiness, but know that it is not to be found where you seek it; you seek a blessed life in the region of death, but it is not to be found there, for how should there be a blessed life found, where there is not so much as life found?" And elsewhere, speaking to God, he says, "All things are full of trouble and difficulty, and You alone are rest and happiness." Truly the creature (as Solomon tells us) is nothing else but vanity and vexation of spirit; but in God there is rest, there is happiness, there is satisfaction of soul to be found; and if you would be happy indeed, choose Him, and place your rest and happiness in Him alone.

5. Consider that God freely offers Himself as an unchangeable good in His covenant to you. You know how He speaks to sinners, even to sinners.

"Come unto Me, and I will make an everlasting covenant with you" (Isaiah 55:3). And pray, what is this covenant? Why, "I will be your God" (Jeremiah 31:33), that you know as the grand promise of it. In the covenant God offers Himself to sinners in all His glorious excellencies and perfections. His language therein to them is, "Come, souls, see what a God I am, how great, how good, how rich, how glorious; see what treasures of light and life, of love and glory there are in Me; and lo! I am willing to be yours, your God, your friend, your Father, your portion, your happiness, your all forever. Look whatever I am, that I will be to you; and whatever I can do, that I will do for you."

Thus He offers Himself in all His glorious excellencies and perfections to you, and as in all, so particularly in His unchangeableness. "Come," says He, "I am the Lord, I change not, and as such a one do I tender Myself to you. My unchangeableness shall be the rock of your rest; the immutability of My nature, My counsel, My covenant, My love, is a sure footing for your faith, and a firm foundation for your comfort. As long as I exist, I will be life and blessedness to you; I will be a never-failing fountain of peace, joy, and satisfaction to you. 'I am the first and the last, He who was, and is, and is to come,' and as such I will be yours forever; and when the world and all that is therein shall be burned up, I will be a standing portion for you; when the whole world is like a tumbling ocean round about you, I will be a Rock of Ages to you; and be not afraid of Me, for I am a God of grace and love. It is true, I am the 'great and high God,' but My highness shall stoop, and My

greatness shall condescend to you; yes, and nothing
shall stand between you and Me, no sin, no vileness,
no unworthiness of yours. I know you are poor, vile,
sinful, worthless worms, infinitely unworthy of Me; I
know your sins are many, and the distance between
Me and you is great; but all this shall not hinder you
from an interest in Me and My unchangeableness, if
you will take hold of My covenant, choose Me for
your God and portion, and take up the rest and happiness of your souls in Me."

Thus God reveals and offers Himself in His
covenant to us; and does He thus offer Himself in
His covenant to us, and shall we not choose Him for
our God and portion? Shall we stick in the creature
still and reject the offer God makes of Himself to us?
God forbid! Oh, let us now choose this unchangeable God, and let Him be our rest, our portion, our
happiness, and our all forever.

Let us reason matters a little in our own souls.
The world is full of changes, and all my creature
comforts and contentments are subject to change. I
am not sure of them one moment, my own last and
great change is near at hand, I know not how soon
it will come upon me, and nothing but the unchangeable God can make me happy; and He freely
offers Himself in His covenant to me; and shall I yet,
notwithstanding all this, neglect Him? Shall I cleave
to the creature, and not to this unchangeable God?
By no means; He, not the fading, dying creature,
shall be my portion and my happiness forever. Or, if
all this does not persuade, then once more:

6. Consider how sad and dreadful a thing it will
be to have the unchangeableness of God against

you. This is a sure rule, that unless we make God ours by choosing Him, and by closing in His covenant with Him as our God and portion, He and all His attributes will at last be found against us to destroy us and make us miserable forever. If we make not God's unchangeableness ours, and engage it not for us, by choosing Him as unchangeable, His unchangeableness will stand forever engaged against us; and oh, how sad that will be! It is sad to have any attribute of God against man; but to have His unchangeableness against us how sad is that! Oh, for a man to have God for his eternal enemy, God eternally and unchangeably set against him, this is enough to render him completely and unchangeably miserable!

Again, therefore, let me call upon you to look and live above changeable creatures, and to choose, rest in, and live upon the unchangeable God as your God and portion. Look upon Him in Christ, in whom you will find Him infinitely full of love and sweetness, in whom you will find Him to be love itself. "God is love" (1 John 4:8). Accordingly, let your souls choose Him, and cleave to Him, as yours forever.

Chapter Ten

We are to imitate God, and labor for a likeness to Him in His unchangeableness, by being more constant in that which is good; this, in some measure, is attainable in this world; it is near the life of heaven

Unchangeableness being one of the glorious excellencies and perfections of God, why should we not imitate Him? Why should we not labor to be like Him herein? Why should we not covet and press after a holy unchangeableness in our spirits and walkings with Him? Sure I am, it is what His unchangeableness calls upon us for. "From the consideration of God's immutability (said a learned man), it follows that we also should labor to be immutable in the things of God—in faith, in hope, in love, and the like." As the consideration of God's holiness calls for holiness in us, and the consideration of His goodness and mercy calls for goodness and mercy in us, and the consideration of His patience calls for patience in us, so the consideration of His unchangeableness calls for a holy unchangeableness, at least something like it: a holy evenness, steadiness, and fixedness of spirit in our ways and walkings with Him and before Him. It calls upon us to be more constant and uniform in all holy obedience, and in the exercise of all grace.

True, my beloved, there are some things so peculiarly appropriate to God that in respect of them there can be no formal likeness in the creature to Him, and it would be impious boldness for any to aspire thereunto. Such things are His supreme dominion and sovereign authority, His absolute independence and self-sufficiency. Now in these, men affect to imitate Him, they wickedly affront Him. But now some other perfections are found in the blessed God, not so incommunicable and appropriate to Him but that His creatures may be said to have some participation thereof with Him, and so far to be truly like Him; such are His holiness, His justice, His mercy, His patience, and the like, wherein it is our duty, as well as our glory, to imitate Him, and to labor for as great a resemblance and as full conformity to Him as possibly we can. Christ commands us to be perfect, "as your Father which is in heaven is perfect" (Matthew 5:48), and we are enjoined to "be followers of God, as dear children" (Ephesians 5:1). The word literally is: "Be imitators of God; be like Him, bearing His image upon you; and if you are His children indeed, you will do so."

We should imitate God in all His imitable excellencies and perfections; yes, observe this moreover, that where there cannot be a proper and formal likeness or similitude in us to God, in respect of those peculiarly appropriate excellencies that are in Him, yet even there should we labor for impressions, affections, dispositions, and demeanors of soul towards Him, suitable and answerable to those excellencies and perfections of His. For instance, He being absolutely supreme, there ought to be in us a

humble subjection and self-resignation of soul, dis-
posing us to constant obedience to Him. He being
simply and absolutely independent and self-suffi-
cient, there ought to be in us a self-emptiness and
nothingness, living wholly and entirely out of ourselves upon Him as such a God, fetching all from
His fountain of fullness. Thus were we not capable
of any formal likeness to God, we should yet study
His perfections, and labor for dispositions of spirit
and demeanors of soul suitable thereunto. But
where we are capable of any likeness to Him, there
we should covet it and press after it. God therefore
being unchangeable, we should labor for a holy unchangeableness in our spirits and walkings before
Him; we should imitate Him, and conform to Him
herein, so far as we are capable of so doing. We
should labor for more fixedness, more evenness,
more constancy and uniformity in all grace and holiness, in all heavenliness and obedience, in all acts
of duty and walking with God.

It is what, in a good measure, may be attained
unto even here in this world. It is possible, my
beloved, for these roving, inconstant, unstable souls
of ours to be in some good measure brought up to a
holy evenness and unchangeableness in the ways
and things of God; for this is what some of the
saints have attained unto. It is said of Enoch that
"he walked with God three hundred years, and begat
sons and daughters" (Genesis 5:22). Of others it is
said that they begat such and such, and they lived so
many years afterwards. But of Enoch it is said, "he
begat Methuselah, and walked with God three hundred years," as if his whole life for those three hun-

dred years were one continued and uninterrupted course of walking with God. The phrase (as a learned critic observed) seems to carry this in it: "He had God so present always with him, and he so accommodated himself to the pleasure of God, that he seemed perpetually to walk with Him." His life was, as it were, one constant course and series of walking with Him. This also is what God calls for: "Be steadfast, immovable, always abounding in the work of the Lord" (1 Corinthians 15:58). This is what the apostles are ever and soon praying for, both for themselves and others: "The God of all grace establish, strengthen, settle you" (1 Peter 5:10). This is what, being attained, is the crown and perfection of a Christian; so, as that verse states more fully, "The God of all grace, after you have suffered a while, make you perfect, establish, strengthen you."

To be established, and settled in our spirits and ways in holy things, is our perfection. It is indeed the glory of Christianity and the honor of a Christian. O my beloved, the more even and uniform we are in the things and ways of God, the more excellent and perfect we are, and the more amiable in the sight of God. Oh, it is not the flashy, high-flown talking, but the even and steady Christian who is most excellent, most amiable in God's eye. This is a crown of glory indeed upon the head of a poor soul.

It was Queen Elizabeth's motto: "always the same." And truly, were it more in a holy respect the Christian's motto, he would be more glorious than he is. "Rawlins you left me, and Rawlins you find me," said that martyr, meaning that he was still of the same mind, the same spirit, being constant to his testimony, which was his crown and glory.

"It is a high and great thing (said one to his friend) which you desire, and even bordering upon a deity, not to be moved and changed." Sure I am, it is a high and great thing in spiritual matters to come up to a holy evenness and fixedness of soul. This is that which honors the gospel; this is that which renders religion amiable; this is that which makes way for full and constant communion with God, for abiding consolations; this is that which delights the heart of God; this is that which brings us near to the state and life of heaven; for there the saints and angels are fixed and unchangeably confirmed in all good, in all holiness, in all happiness.

Oh, labor for as much of this holy unchangeableness as possibly may be attained unto here on earth, and then sigh and long for that life and state where you shall know no change forever, but be perfectly, unchangeably, and eternally holy and happy, as God Himself is, for you shall be like Him, "and see Him as He is" (1 John 3:2). It is true, it is no easy thing to fix our roving spirits, and reduce them to a steadiness in what is good; but remember the God you are to have recourse to, to do this great work for you, is "the God of all grace" (1 Peter 5:10), as we have previously quoted, and He therefore can do it with ease for you. Oh, look to Him for this great blessing, this high attainment.

Chapter Eleven

The unchangeableness of God a sweet spring of comfort to His people; several consolatory conclusions thence

As God's unchangeableness calls for much duty, so it ministers much sweet comfort to His poor church and people. The truth is, there is scarcely any such spring and treasury of comfort as this is. "God's immutability (said one) is the best cordial to refresh a fainting soul." The great cordial God sent Israel in their distress was this: "I AM THAT I AM" (Exodus 3:14), or "I am an unchangeable God"; and indeed that was enough for them. But more particularly there are several consolatory conclusions which flow from God's unchangeableness, conclusions which carry strong consolation in them:

1. God being unchangeable, His glory shall live and in due time shine forth conspicuously before all. See this in these words: "I am the Lord, I am Jehovah" (Isaiah 42:8); that is, "I am He who was, and is, and is to come." He is the unchangeable God; and what then? Why, "My glory will I not give to another, nor My praise to graven images." In other words, "My glory shall not die but live, My glory shall not be always veiled and eclipsed; but it shall shine forth in perfect luster and splendor."

One of the great burdens that lie upon the peo-

ple of God is the sufferings of His name and glory.
"The reproaches of them that reproached Thee are
fallen upon me," said David in Psalm 69:9. God's
glory is veiled. His name is blasphemed. His worship
is interrupted. His providence is denied, all His attributes are obscured, and His honor is in every way
thrown in the dust, which makes holy souls go
mourning from day to day. But, my beloved, here is
that which may comfort the soul: God is unchangeable, and therefore His glory shall live and shine
forth again. The veil shall in due time be taken
away, and His glory shall appear; yes, it shall be as
eminently illustrated and displayed as ever it has
been veiled and eclipsed.

You know how God speaks in reference to the
glory of His name in answer to Christ's prayer:
"Father, glorify Thy name" (John 12:28). What answer does the Father give Him? "I have glorified it,
and I will glorify it again." That is, "I have hitherto
taken care of My glory, and I will take care of it still."
O my beloved, God's glory has hitherto been dear to
Him, and He has hitherto maintained it in the
world, and He is unchangeable, and therefore His
glory is as dear to Him as ever it was. He is as jealous
for it as ever. He is also every bit as able to vindicate
and maintain it as ever He was. Assure yourselves,
were it not that He knows how to make it shine
forth so much the more illustriously and conspicuously afterwards, He would not suffer it to be so
veiled and eclipsed as sometimes He does. Yes, let
me say that He is always carrying on—as the interest
of His people's happiness, so the concerns of His
own glory.

2. God being unchangeable, His church shall be preserved and delivered—preserved under, and in due time delivered out of, all her troubles and afflictions; and what a sweet thing is that! The poor church of God is oftentimes plunged into very deep and sore distress, such as are ready to sink and overwhelm her. She is oftentimes "afflicted, tossed with tempests, and not comforted" (Isaiah 54:11). Such indeed is her condition at this day; and as good old "Eli sat trembling for the ark of God" (1 Samuel 4:13), a type of the church, so it may be that some may now sit trembling for the Church of God, fearing how it will go with her; and indeed he is not one of Zion's children, that is not concerned for Zion's afflictions. But lo! my beloved, in the midst of all such fears and tremblings of heart, there is strong consolation. God is unchangeable, and, being unchangeable, He will certainly support and deliver His Church, and that in the best way and fittest season.

God has never yet failed His Church in her afflictions. Yes, it is admirable to consider how hitherto He has carried it towards her under all her distress; how sweetly He has supported her, and how seasonably He has delivered her. When they were in Egypt in the iron furnace; when they were in the wilderness; when they were in the Red Sea; when they were in Babylon, in Haman's time and in Herod's time; when the neck of the whole Church of God was upon the block at once, as it were, and also all down, through the times of anti-christian tyranny and persecution to this very day, oh, how admirably has God wrought for them in supporting and delivering them! And, certainly, what He has done, that He can and will do for them again as the case shall require. God is unchangeable. "His hand is not shortened, that He cannot save; nor His ear grown heavy, that He cannot hear" (Isaiah 59:1).

God being unchangeable, He is as tender of, and careful for, His Church and people as ever He was. Being unchangeable, He is in every way the same to His people now as He was formerly; the same in His love to them, His jealousy for them, His sympathy with them, and His interest in them. He stands in the same covenant relation to them as ever He did. He is their King, their Head, their Husband, their Friend, their Father, their Shepherd, now as well as heretofore. He is in every way as able to help them, and accordingly will support and, in due time, deliver them; and faith sees and rests assured of this. "Awake, awake, put on strength, O arm of the Lord; awake, as in the ancient days, in the generations of old; art Thou not it that hath cut Rahab, and wounded the dragon? Art Thou not it which hath dried the sea, the waters of the great deep; that hath made the depths of the sea a way for the ransomed to pass over?" (Isaiah 51:9–10). So again, "But we had the sentence of death in ourselves, but in God who raiseth the dead, who delivered us from so great a death, and doth deliver; in whom we trust that He will yet deliver us" (2 Corinthians 1:9–10).

Mark, faith, you see, argues from what God has done to what He will do for His poor Church and people; and what ground has it to do so but His unchangeableness? Let Zion, therefore, the Church and people of God, take heed of that language which they spoke of old: "Zion said, 'The Lord hath forsaken me, and my God hath forgotten me' " (Isaiah 49:14). Or as Jacob elsewhere said, "My way is hid from the Lord, and my judgement is passed over by my God." But God must change, if this were to be. True, God may permit His Church to be sorely afflicted, as at this day, but it is but to illustrate His own glory the more in her support and deliverance.

3. God being unchangeable, His enemies shall be destroyed; they shall all die and perish. I mean His incorrigible, implacable enemies who will not stoop to the scepter of His kingdom. God may, and sometimes does, permit His and His people's enemies to practice and prosper, and for a long time together He lets them alone in their sins and oppositions against both Himself and them; yes, He even "fills their belly with His hid treasure" (as you have it in Psalm 17:14). He lets them enjoy some of the best of outward comforts and contentments, and that in great fullness, which oftentimes proves a great burden and temptation to His poor, afflicted people, such as are ready to sin and bear them down.

So it was with the psalmist in Psalm 73, and it is so many times with us; but remember that God is unchangeable, and, being unchangeable, though He may permit His and His people's enemies to practice and prosper for a time, yet not always. No, they shall be destroyed, and that with a great destruction. Pray observe how things issued at last in that very psalm: "Surely Thou didst set them in slippery places, Thou castest them down into destruction; how are they brought into desolation as in a moment! They are utterly consumed with terrors"

(Psalm 73:18–19). Pray observe, he was not more offended at, nor was he more ready to envy their prosperity before, than now he wonders at their ruin and
destruction. "I have seen the wicked in great power,
and spreading himself like a green bay tree, yet he
passed away, and lo! he was not. Yea, I sought him,
but he could not be found; the transgressors shall
be destroyed together; the end of the wicked shall be
cut off" (Psalm 37:35–38). God says, in reference to
His and His people's enemies, "To Me belongeth
vengeance and recompense; their foot shall slide in
due time, for the day of their calamity is at hand,
and the things which shall come upon them make
haste, for the Lord shall judge His people"
(Deuteronomy 32:35–36). Still, you see, though God
permits His and His people's enemies to prosper for
a time, yet at last they are destroyed; and as sure as
God is unchangeable, they shall be destroyed.

Pray, compare my text for this book with the
verse immediately preceding: " 'I will come near to
you to judgment (says God), and I will be a swift witness against the sorcerers, and against the adulter-
ers, and against false swearers, and against all that
oppress the hireling in his wages, the widow and the
fatherless, and that fear not Me,' saith the Lord"
(Malachi 3:5). "I will suddenly and terribly destroy
all My enemies, all that go on in their sinning
against Me." But how shall we be assured of this? He
tells you in the next words, for "I am the Lord, I
change not." It is as if He had said, "As sure as I am
God and unchangeable, they shall be destroyed."

O sirs, though God permits His and His people's
enemies to prosper for a time, yet He always cer-

tainly destroys them in the conclusion, and He will
do so still, because He is unchangeable. God is in
every way the same as ever He was, the same in holiness, jealousy, justice, power, that ever He was. He is
as holy now as ever He was, and so hates sin as much
as ever He did. He is as just now as ever He was, and
so as ready and disposed to take vengeance as ever.
He is as jealous now, as jealous for His name, worship, gospel, and people, as ever He was, and so will
as little bear with the opposers and abusers of them.
He is as wise and powerful now as ever, and so as
able to deal with His enemies. It is a great Scripture
that says, "He is wise in heart, and mighty in
strength; who ever hardened himself against Him
and prospered?" (Job 9:4). Oh, never any yet did, and
never any shall. No, but "He will wound the head of
His enemies, and the hairy scalp of such a one as
goeth on still in his trespasses" (Psalm 68:21). Oh,
that all the enemies of God and His people, and all
rebellious, impenitent ones, would lay this to heart.

4. God being unchangeable, the purposes and
promises of His grace to His Church and people
shall certainly be accomplished. God's heart, my
beloved, has been full of counsels and purposes of
love toward His people from all eternity, and He has
also made many blessed promises to them,
"promises that are exceeding great and precious"
(2 Peter 1:4), because they are full of exceedingly
great and precious things. Greatness and preciousness do not often meet together; many things are
great, but then they are not precious; and many
things are precious, but then they are not great. But
in the promises of God to His Church and people,

greatness and preciousness meet.

Now, whatever purposes God has had in His heart, and whatever promises He has made in this world to His people, they shall all be accomplished because He is an unchangeable God. He is the same now as He was when He took up those purposes and made those promises, and therefore will assuredly make them all good in due season. And so much He tells us: "I am God, and there is none else. I am God, and there is none like Me, declaring the end from the beginning, and from ancient times the things that are not yet done, saying, 'My counsel shall stand, and I will do all my pleasure.' I have spoken, and I will bring it to pass; I have purposed it, I also will do it" (Isaiah 46:9–11).

Mark, first He asserts His Godhead and unchangeableness, and then He tells you all His pleasure shall stand and be accomplished. God being unchangeable, first, none can turn Him or make Him alter His mind. "He is in one mind, and who can turn Him? And what His soul desireth, even that He doeth, for He performeth the thing that is appointed for me" (Job 23:13–14). The wisest and most resolved among men may possibly be wrought upon, and brought over from what they purposed; but it is not so with God.

Second, none can hinder Him from or in His making good His purposes and promises. "Before the day was, I am He, and there is none that can deliver out of My hand. I will work, and who shall let it?" (Isaiah 43:13). Poor soul, whoever you are, who are one of the Lord's people, look back to the eternal counsels and purposes of His love towards you,

and you will find them a great deep, a fountain of
infinite sweetness. In them you will see heaps of love
and treasures of grace; and then turn your eye to the
promises of His covenant, which you will find inex-
pressibly sweet and exactly suitable to your condition, to all your wants, and then know assuredly that
the whole, both of the one and the other, shall be
accomplished to you in due season. It is true indeed,
His counsels may seem to us to be frustrated, and
His promises may for a time be deferred and de-
layed, insomuch that our hasty unbelieving hearts
may be ready to conclude that they will never be accomplished, saying with the psalmist, "Does His
promise fail for evermore?" (Psalm 77:8). But, soul,
wait a while, and they shall all be made good to a tittle.

Has He promised to pardon you, to cleanse you,
to give you a new heart and a new spirit, and to write
His law in your heart? Has He promised to save you
and lodge you at last in His own bosom? Then know
it shall all be accomplished. Oh, how sweet is this!
Oh, to fasten upon a promise and see it surely to be
made good, as in God's unchangeableness we may.
There we may see all as sure, as if it were already accomplished. Oh, what strong consolation does this
afford! What inexpressible sweetness will this give
unto a soul!

5. God being unchangeable, the saints are unchangeably happy, and have a blessed asylum to flee
unto under all those changes and emergencies that
may at any time come upon them. Pray mark, my
beloved, God is the saints' God and portion. And in
Him their happiness lies. He therefore being un-

changeable, they have an unchangeable happiness; they are a happy people, and they will be unchangeably so. "The counsel of the Lord standeth forever, the thoughts of His heart to all generations"; and what then? "Blessed is the nation whose God is the Lord, and the people whom He hath chosen for His own inheritance" (Psalm 33:11–12).

The saints (as one well observed) are in all respects a blessed people. They are blessed in the pardon of their sins: "Blessed is the man whose sins are forgiven" (Psalm 32:1). They are blessed in regard to the disposition of their souls: "Blessed are the poor in spirit, blessed are the meek, blessed are they that hunger and thirst after righteousness" (Matthew 5:3, 5–6). They are blessed in their obedience and walking with God: "Blessed are the undefiled in the way" (Psalm 119:1). They are blessed in their hopes and expectations: "Blessed are they that wait for God" (Isaiah 30:18). Thus they are in every way, and in all respects, a blessed people; but here lies the perfection and crowning glory of their blessedness, and what indeed comprehends all the rest in it, namely, that the unchangeable God is their God and portion. "Happy is the people whose God is the Lord" (Psalm 144:15). Oh, this speaks them to be infinitely and unchangeably happy, and accordingly they should live upon Him, and that under all their strains and difficulties.

Oh, sirs, what is there that this will not support and comfort you under? Do your friends and comforts here change? However, God, your best friend and comfort, changes not, and that is enough. Do times and seasons change, and that for the worse,

from sunshine to storms? Well, however, soul, your
God changes not, and that is enough to sweeten all.
Do you yourself change? Changes and war are upon
you, and, which is the worst of it, your spirit
changes; it will not keep even with God one hour.
Well, still your God changes not, and that is
enough. Do new temptations arise and old corrup-
tions break out anew? Does guilt revive and recur
upon you? Be it so, yet your God is unchangeable,
and so can and will relieve and succor you now as
well as formerly, and that is enough.

Yes, do God's dispensations change towards you?
He did smile, now He frowns. He did lift up, now He
casts down. The light of His countenance did shine
brightly upon you, now it is veiled and clouded.
However, your God Himself changes not: His heart,
His counsel, His covenant, and His love are still the
same towards you as ever they were, howbeit the dispensation is changed. Oh, this one word, "God is
mine, and He is unchangeable," has infinite sweetness in it, and it speaks me to be infinitely and unchangeably happy. Oh, you who are the people of
God, labor to see and rejoice in this happiness of
yours. That you may the better do this, let me add
only two short words to this, and I will close the
whole discourse:

First, consider that as your God is unchangeable,
so you are unchangeably interested in Him. This
unchangeable God is unchangeably your God.

However, though God is unchangeable, some
poor soul may say, "What will that avail me? My interest in Him, I fear, will change and fail; there will
be shortly an end of that."

No, soul, the unchangeable God being indeed yours, He is yours forever. So the church said, "This God is our God forever and ever" (Psalm 48:14). O soul, you, through infinite, free, and rich grace, have a covenant interest in and relation to the unchangeable God, and this interest and relation of yours is a firm, lasting, and unchangeable interest and relation. Nothing that either men, devils, or lusts can do can possibly break or crack it.

I shall here only add a saying or two of Augustine. "The chief good, which is God, is neither given to such as are unwilling to have Him, nor taken away from such as are unwilling to part with Him." And elsewhere, "No man does or can lose Thee, O God, unless he is willing to lose Thee and go without Thee. And he that willingly parts with Thee, whither does he go? Whither does he flee, but from Thee smiling to Thee frowning; from Thee a reconciled Father to Thee an angry judge?"

Oh, soul, as long as you are willing to have God as yours, so long He shall be yours; yes, more, your interest in Him depends not upon your willingness for it, but upon His unchangeable love and covenant; and His love and covenant both must change before your interest in Him can fade and change.

Second, consider, as your God is unchangeable, so after a while you shall unchangeably enjoy Him and be with Him; your vision and fruition of Him shall be unchangeable. "Our happiness (said Augustine) is begun here in election, but it is perfected hereafter in fruition." You who have chosen the unchangeable God, you shall, after a few days, enjoy the God whom you have chosen; your happiness is great in your choosing of Him, but how much more great will it be in your enjoying of Him! "Thou shalt guide me by Thy counsels, and afterwards receive me unto glory; whom have I in heaven but Thee? and there is none upon earth that I desire besides Thee" (Psalm 73:24–25). "I have chosen, and I do again choose Thee for my God and portion. Some enjoyment I have of Thee here, and more I shall have hereafter in heaven. I shall ere long be taken to enjoy Thee in Thy glory, fully, immediately, and forever, for Thou art mine, and I have made a solemn choice of Thee."

O saints! The unchangeable God is yours, and some communion you have with Him here in the ways of His grace, which is sweet and happy, but after you have enjoyed Him in the ways of His grace a while here, you shall be taken to the unchangeable enjoyment of Him in His glory above, which will be infinitely more sweet and happy. Your enjoyment of Him here is low and remote, as well as changeable and inconstant; but your enjoyment of Him above will be full, close, and unchangeable.

Here you have, now and then, a gracious visit from Him. He visits you in this duty and that ordinance, in this mercy and in that affliction; but, oh, how short many times are those visits of His! Alas! He is gone again in a moment. But after a while you shall enjoy Him in His glory, and there you shall not have a short visit now and then only, but His constant presence forever. "We shall be ever with the Lord" (1 Thessalonians 4:17).

O blessed souls! There He will unchangeably de-

light in you, unchangeably shine upon you, unchangeably communicate Himself in His grace and
glory to you. Oh, how sweet and blessed will this be!

Well, to close all. Saints, the unchangeable God
is unchangeably your God, and howbeit your visions
of Him are yet but dark, and your communion with
Him but low, yet wait a while and the day will break,
and all your shadows shall flee away. You shall ex-
change your ebbing waters for a full tide, your
glimmerings and dawnings for a noonday, your imperfect beginnings for a full and perfect consumma-
tion of communion with Him. Howbeit there is now
a veil upon His face so that you cannot behold Him,
yet wait a while and the veil shall be taken away, and
you shall behold His face, His glory forever; and that
so as to be fully changed into the image thereof, and
eternally solaced and satisfied therein, suitable to
that word.

I shall close all with this: "As for me, I will behold Thy face in righteousness; I shall be satisfied,
when I awake, with Thy likeness" (Psalm 17:15).
Amen.

The Soul's Rest in God

Opened and improved from Psalm 116:7:
"Return unto thy rest, O my soul."

Chapter One

An introduction to the words; what that rest is which David calls on his soul to return unto; the sum of the words and our intention from them laid down in one general position

It is the great happiness of the saints that, though they meet with many sore troubles and afflictions here in this world, yes, though they meet with little else *but* trouble and affliction here, yet there is a rest to come for them—a sweet rest, a blessed rest, a glorious rest, a rest not liable to decay or disturbance forever. So the Apostle tells us: "There remaineth a rest to the people of God" (Hebrews 4:9). Nor is this all their happiness, for not only does there remain a rest for them hereafter, but there is also a rest, a sweet rest, a blessed rest, which they do or may attain unto here—a rest even in the midst of all those troubles which here they are exposed unto. And blessed be God for this rest.

Rest is sweet, but rest in trouble, rest in the midst of many and sore troubles, oh, how sweet, how glorious is this! Now this is the rest which I would briefly contemplate and speak to, as the proper subject of these words in Psalm 116:7: "Return unto thy rest, O my soul." These words are David's call or command to his soul to return unto its rest. And the only thing to be inquired into for the exposition of them, and therein for making way to what we intend from them, is what this rest is which David here calls upon his soul to return unto. I find it expounded in two ways:

1. Some expound it of God Himself, God in Christ, who indeed is the rest as well as the refuge of His people. God is the center of quiet (as the schoolmen say), the proper, quieting, resting center of the soul, and in Him alone can it truly rest. Thus a learned man expounds it, "Return to Him in whom you will find the most perfect rest; to wit, unto God." Indeed, with Him and in Him alone is perfect rest to be found, as in its place may be shown.

2. Others expound it of a quiet, serene, sedate, well-composed frame and posture of soul; and thus Calvin and others expound it: "That some interpreters do by rest here understand God is strained; it is rather to be taken for a tranquil and well-composed frame of soul." And indeed the scope of the context looks this way, for, mark it, David had been in great affliction. The sorrows of death had compassed him about, and the pains of hell had gotten hold upon him, as you find in verse 3, and hereupon there had followed, as is too probable, great perplexity of spirit within, great murmurings and tumults, frettings and discomposures in his soul; and now he calls off his soul from those unquiet motions and agitations, and commands it to return to rest, that is, to a calm, quiet, serene, sedate, and well-composed frame again.

Thus also another judicious interpreter expounds it, as if David should say, "O my soul, hitherto you have been tossed up and down, among the

waves and storms of sorrows, doubts and despera-
tion; you have been greatly afflicted and disturbed,
when the sorrows of death and hell pressed in upon
you. Sometimes such has been the case with you that
you could see no port, no haven in which you might
rest. But now these storms are over and gone, and a
port has opened itself to your faith in which you may
rest; now put in, and return to your rest. Now be
quiet and joyful, knowing where you ought to rest."

Thus this rest is doubly expounded. I shall exclude neither of these senses, but rather join them
both together, and by "rest" here understand the
souls being at rest in God, in whom alone rest is to
be found for souls. Nor am I alone in so doing; for I
find a learned man so to understand it: "Be no
longer filled with disquietude and perturbation, but
acquiesce and sit down satisfied in God, your rest
and portion forever."

Accordingly take the sum of the whole, and so of
my intention in this position:

**DOCTRINE. The souls of the saints should be at
rest in God, or, the frame and posture of soul the
saints should live in is a frame and posture of rest in
God.**

Whatever the saints' condition may be, or whatever dispensations they may be exercised with, yet
their souls should be at rest in God. David's soul was
for a time gone off its rest; it was gone from the se-
dateness, composure, and satisfaction which it was
wont to have in God. His condition was full of trouble and disturbance, and his soul was filled with
trouble and disturbance too; but here, tacitly at least,
he rebukes his soul for this, and expressly com-

mands it to return to rest again, to a rest in God, and that as its proper posture. Mark how he speaks: "Return unto thy rest, O my soul." The proper posture of the souls of the saints is to be at rest in God, and that posture they should be in at all times and in all conditions. What the soul's rest in God is, what obligations the saints are under to be thus at rest in God, the sweetness and excellency of the frame, with a call to live in this frame and posture, and helps in order thereunto, are the things which will properly fall under consideration as we proceed in this argument.

Chapter Two

*What the soul's rest in God is, opened, and when
the soul may be said to be at rest in Him*

But what is it for a soul to be at rest in God or to
live in a posture of rest in God? In general, it is for a
soul to sit down satisfied with what God does as best,
and with what God is as all. So this rest of the soul in
God lies in two things: first, in a free and cheerful
submission to the divine will and providence; second, in a full and ample satisfaction in and with the
divine presence and fullness. And, oh, the beauty,
the sweetness, the amiableness that both these carry
in them! A little about each:

1. It is to sit down satisfied with what God does as
best, and so it lies in a free and cheerful submission
to the divine will and providence, the will and providence of God concerning oneself. The soul,
through grace, gets right apprehensions of God's
will and providence concerning him. He looks
upon the will of God to be a sovereign, righteous,
wise, and good will, and hereupon he sits down satisfied with it—whatever it does with him, whatever it
allots and orders out concerning him.

(1) The soul looks upon the will and providence of God concerning him to be a sovereign will
and providence, a will and providence which does
and which may do with him whatever it pleases; and

so he acquiesces in it. "It is the Lord (said good old Eli), let Him do what seemeth Him good" (1 Samuel 3:18). Mark how he bows and submits his soul to the divine will and providence: "It is the Lord; it is a sovereign God, a God who may do with me and mine whatever He will." And in the sense of this his soul freely submits.

It was a dreadful and terrible message which Samuel told Eli from the Lord; but as dreadful and terrible as it was, yet having his eye upon the sovereignty of God Eli freely acquiesced. Suitable thereunto is the observation of a learned man upon this place: "Eli in these words expresses great patience, and a great contentment or agreement with the divine will. He did not expostulate with God, but humbly, completely comported with Him." God, my beloved, has an absolute sovereignty over us all, and may do with us as He pleases. It is what He claims for Himself as His prerogative: "All souls are mine" (Ezekiel 18:4). "They are mine to do with them, to dispose of them, as I will." As you know, God asserts His sovereignty in these words: "O house of Israel, cannot I do with you as this potter? Behold, as the clay is in the potter's hand, so are ye in My hand, O house of Israel" (Jeremiah 18:6). Pray, mark, He had already (verse 4) shown them how the potter dealt with the clay, and what an absolute power He had over it, making it a vessel and marring it again as He pleased. Now here in verse 6 He says, "Cannot I do with you as this potter does with his clay? I can. Behold, as the clay is in the hand of the potter, so are you in My hand. I have an absolute power over you, to do with you and dispose of you as I see good, and I may make or mar you upon the wheel of My providence as I please."

And you know how God, by the Apostle, argues in that greatest of cases: "Hath not the potter power over the clay, of the same lump to make one vessel unto honor, and another unto dishonor?" (Romans 9:21). In these words God asserts His absolute sovereignty to dispose of all men, as to their eternal state, as He pleases. Thus He has an absolute sovereignty over all. Now the holy soul, apprehending this sovereignty in God, falls under the awe and dread of it and accordingly acquiesces in His will, whatever it is.

(2) The soul looks upon the will and providence of God concerning him to be a holy and righteous, as well as a sovereign, will and providence, and upon that account also acquiesces therein. "The Lord is righteous (said the church in Lamentations 1:18), for I have rebelled against His commandment." In other words, "It is true, my sorrow is great and my affliction heavy, but God is just and holy in it. It is not more than, nor, in truth, as much as my sins have deserved." Indeed, God's dealings with her were very terrible and amazing, but yet, apprehending the righteousness of God in them, she submitted to Him under all. "O Lord, righteousness belongeth unto Thee, but unto us confusion of face" (Daniel 9:7). They saw the righteousness of God in His dealings with them, and so were at rest in His will. God is righteous (the Scripture tells us) in all His ways, and holy in all His works, and He is a just Lord that doth, that can do, no wrong, no iniquity (Zephaniah 3:5).

Now the holy soul gets a sight of this, is awed with the sense thereof, and, accordingly, acquiesces in God's will. "True (says he), this and that is sharp; it smarts sorely; it runs counter to my carnal appetite, to my sense and reason; but I am sure God is holy and just in all. I have deserved all and more at His hands." And in the sense of this he acquiesces in His will and is satisfied with His dealings.

(3) The soul looks upon the will and providence of God concerning him to be a wise as well as a holy will and providence, and thereupon also bows to it and acquiesces in it. God, my beloved, is the only wise God, and all His works are done in wisdom. His will is a wise will, a will guided and ordered by counsel. He "works all things according to the counsel of His own will" (Ephesians 1:11). God is never out of character in what He does, but does all as becomes an only and an infinitely wise God. In this, the holy soul, getting a sight and sense of God's wisdom, freely acquiesces in whatever the will of God is concerning him, and rests fully satisfied with what God does. We read that "in all this Job sinned not, neither charged he God foolishly" (Job 1:22).

"In all this"—in all his trials and afflictions, though many, though great—"in all this Job sinned not, neither charged he God foolishly"; or, as you have it in the margin of some of your Bibles, "he did not attribute folly to God." He sinned not by attributing folly to God; but he worshipped and adored the divine wisdom, the wisdom of God in all His dealings with him. He acquitted God's providence of folly, bowed to the infinite wisdom thereof, and was satisfied with all as best for him. "All this," says the holy soul, "is the work of a wise will, regulated by counsel; true, all runs cross to my will and my outward interest, but it is all balanced by infinite wisdom, and I am satisfied therewith." Thus he is at rest in God.

(4) The soul looks upon the will and providence of God concerning him to be a good, as well as a wise, will and providence, and thus also acquiesces in it. The psalmist tells us that "all the paths of the Lord are mercy and truth to such as keep His covenant and His testimonies" (Psalm 25:10). By "the paths of the Lord" here we are to understand His providences. Now, says he, these are all mercy and truth to His people—not some, but all of them, even the hardest and severest, the most dark, terrible, and killing of them; they are all mercy and truth, mercy itself and truth itself. Whatever the will and providence of God brings forth, yet to His people there is love in all, goodness in all, faithfulness in all. And the holy soul, getting a sight hereof, sweetly acquiesces and is at rest in whatever God does. So David says, "I know, O Lord, that Thy judgments are right, and that Thou in faithfulness hast afflicted me" (Psalm 119:75). See Hezekiah also, speaking to Isaiah: "Good is the word of the Lord which thou hast spoken" (Isaiah 39:8). It was a sharp and severe word or message which God, by Isaiah, sent him, as you may see in the preceding verses. Yet he saw goodness and kindness in all, and accordingly acquiesced therein.

Truly there is love and goodness in all God's dealings with His people, and, the holy soul seeing it, his language is: "Whether God fills or empties, whether He gives or takes away, whether He lifts up or casts down, whether He kills or makes alive—yet there is love in all, goodness in all, and it is best for me. God chooses for me, and disposes for me better than I could for myself, and I am satisfied with what He does." Thus the soul gets right apprehensions of the will and providence of God concerning him, hereupon is sweetly satisfied, and sits down at rest in God in the midst of all He does to him or with him.

True, God may deal somewhat severely with him. He may break him with breach upon breach, as He did Job. He may cause all His waves and His billows to pass over him, as He dealt with David, but still the soul looks upon all to be holy, just, and good, and no other than what God in His sovereignty may do. And so he rests satisfied therewith: he rests contented in God and His will under all. There are no disquietings or perplexities of spirit, no distractions or discomposures of soul; no frettings, no tumults, no murmurings, no risings of heart against God or His will, but there is a sweet calm, serenity, and rest in the soul. He is in a sedate, serene posture in his God; and this rest in God the psalmist speaks of with these words: "Rest in the Lord, and wait patiently for Him; fret not thyself because of him that prospereth in his way" (Psalm 37:7). Resting in God is here opposed to fretting, and so a quiet, sedate, well-composed spirit must rest in God.

2. It is for a soul to sit down satisfied with what God is as all, and so it lies in a full and ample satisfaction in and with the divine presence and fullness. It is for a soul to take up with the blessed God as his

only and all-sufficient portion and happiness forever. God, my beloved, is an all-sufficient God. He
asserts His own all-sufficiency: "I am God all-sufficient" (Genesis 17:1). "I am infinitely sufficient for
Myself, and I am infinitely sufficient for you and all
My people to make the one and the other happy forever."

God is an inexhaustible fountain of light, life,
love, blessedness, perfection and glory. There is all
good in God, and he who has God has all. "To him
that overcometh will I give to inherit all things."
How so? "I will be his God" (Revelation 21:7). He has
all good, all happiness, in Him, and in Him we may
find all as in its fountain-fullness and purity.

Now the soul, seeing God to be such a God, and
withal looking upon Him as his God in covenant,
sits down satisfied with Him alone, saying, "I have
enough. I have all," and so is at rest in Him, whether
he has much or little, anything or nothing of this
world's goods. Whether the streams run high or low
with him, yet here is a fountain of infinite sweetness
and blessedness, and he drinks there and satisfies
himself there. He sees the fountain is so full that he
needs not the streams to make him happy, and accordingly sits down satisfied therewith and is at rest.

Thus David's soul was at rest in God: "The Lord
is the portion of mine inheritance, and of my cup."
Well, what then? Why, he sits down at rest in Him.
"The lines are fallen to me in pleasant places, yea, I
have a goodly heritage" (Psalm 16:5–6). As if to say, "I
have enough, enough for delight, and enough for
satisfaction. I have as much as my soul can wish or
desire." "As for me, I will behold Thy face in righ-

teousness. I shall be satisfied, when I awake, with Thy likeness" (Psalm 17:15). In the verse immediately preceding he had spoken of some whose portion and happiness was in this world.

"Pray, David, where and in what is your portion, your happiness?"

"My portion is in God and my happiness is in God, in the sight of God and in the likeness of God. Let others take up their rest, portion, and happiness where and in what they will; God is my rest, my portion, my happiness, my all forever." Again, "The Lord lives, and blessed be my Rock" (Psalm 18:46). "Such and such comforts are dead and gone; they are not (as Jacob spoke of his sons). But, however, God lives still. I have a living God, and He is a living happiness, and that's enough." So, "Although my house be not so with God, yet He hath made with me an everlasting covenant, ordered in all things, and sure, and this is all my salvation, and all my desire" (2 Samuel 23:5). As if to say, "God is my happiness, even all that my soul can wish." Accordingly, he is at rest in his God. And, "Whom have I in heaven but Thee? and there is none upon earth that I desire in comparison to Thee. My heart and my flesh faileth, but God is the strength of my heart, and my portion forever" (Psalm 73:25–26).

However dark forever things looked with him, yet he, looking to his God, was satisfied and at rest *in* Him and *with* Him, as being infinitely enough *for* him. The prophet Habakkuk resolved upon the same course: "Although the fig tree shall not blossom, neither shall fruit be in the vines; the labor of the olive shall fail . . . yet will I rejoice in the Lord, I will joy in the God of my salvation" (Habakkuk 3: 17–18). He supposes the worst that could come, and yet still resolves to be at rest in God, and that God alone shall be enough for him when all other things fail.

Thus the holy soul sits down satisfied with God alone, setting God, and an interest in Him, over and against all his wants, losses, burdens, difficulties, and temptations, as one infinitely able to relieve and satisfy him under all. His language to God is: "Lord, let others take the Word, and the good things thereof; give me Thyself, and I have enough. Let those run out to broken cisterns who will; let me have a free recourse unto the fountain, and I am satisfied. It is true, the tide of creature comforts runs low with me, and, on the other hand, the waves and surges of affliction rise high; but God is all-sufficient and I have enough in Him." He sees a little of that glorious fullness, sweetness, and blessedness that is in God, and hereupon sings a holy requiem unto himself, saying, "Soul, take your ease; you have goods, light, life, love, blessedness, salvation, enough laid up for you for many days, yes, for the days of eternity. Take your ease, sit down satisfied in and with your God alone; had you ten thousand worlds, without Him you have nothing; but in Him you have all. Rest, therefore, in Him."

Thus you see what it is for a soul to be at rest in God, and when he may be said to be at rest in Him.

Chapter Three

*The great obligations the saints are under thus to
live at rest in God. Several of these obligations
insisted on as the first evidence of the
truth of our proposition*

Now that we have seen what it is for a soul to be
at rest in God, our next work shall be to show you
what obligations the saints are under thus to live at
rest in Him, and that as an undeniable evidence of
the truth of our position. The saints are under
mighty obligations thus to be at rest in God. I shall
insist only on four which are full of weight, and I
beg they may accordingly affect and influence us.

1. The first obligation the saints are under to live
at rest in God is this: the blessed God has freely
made over Himself in His covenant to them, and
that in all His glorious riches and fullness, that in
Him their souls might be at rest. He has given
Himself to them as their rest and portion; and is not
this a mighty obligation in the case? God, my
beloved, in the covenant of His love, has freely given
and made over Himself to His people in all His
riches and fullness, in all His excellencies and perfections, to be used, possessed, and enjoyed by them
as an all-sufficient rest, portion and happiness forever. This is evident in the very tenor of the
covenant, and wherever you have a formal mention

or record of the covenant in Scripture this is put in: "I will be your God."

You have three great and solemn mentions of the covenant in Scripture, and these words are in all of them.. One is Genesis 17:7–8, another is Jeremiah 31:33–34, and the third is in Hebrews 8:10–12. In these places you have the most express records of the covenant, God's covenant with His people, that are in all the Scripture. And in each one there is this: "I will be your God." In the two later places we have other promises, promises of pardon, cleansing, teaching, and the like; but in that to Abraham in Genesis we have only this: "I will be thy God," for, indeed, this comprehends all the rest, and all the other promises that are contained in the covenant of God are but branches growing out of this root, and do but open this to us. This (as one speaks) is the head or top of the covenant. And indeed, when God says to a soul, "I will be your God," He therein says, "I will pardon you. I will cleanse you. I will teach you. I will save you. I will make you happy forever."

For God to be our God is for God to be and communicate all good to us that a God can communicate and creatures receive; it is for God to love us, to bless us, to care for us, to make us happy forever; it is for God to give us eternal life, to be a friend, a father, a husband, and a Savior to us. "It is," as Luther expounded it, "for God to make over Himself in all His excellencies, perfections, and glory—His wisdom, power, goodness, faithfulness, all-sufficiency, unchangeableness, and eternity to His people as their rest and happiness, to be pos-

sessed and enjoyed by them for their good forever."
In a word, for God to say to a poor creature, "I will be
your God," is as much as if He should say, "Look,
whatever I am, that I will be to you; and, look, whatever I *can* do, that I *will* do for you, so far as I am capable of the one or the other to make you happy forever. I am a fountain of life, and such will I be to you.
I am a God of peace and pardon, and such will I be
to you. I am a God of grace and love, yes, I am a God
who is love itself, and such I will be to you. I am the
Father of mercies and the God of all grace, and such
will I be to you. I will beget new mercies for you every
day. I am a God of comfort, yes, of all comfort, and
such will I be to you. I am an unchangeable, eternal,
all-sufficient God, and such will I be to you. I can
pardon guilty souls, break the hardest hearts, en-
lighten the darkest minds, and cleanse the impurest
spirits. I can make unbelieving hearts believing. I
can support drooping spirits, and all this I will do
for you. I can carry you through life and death and
bring you safely to heaven, and there communicate
Myself to you forever, to the filling of your soul with
delight and satisfaction, and this I will do for you."

Surely happy is the soul who has the Lord for his
God, and well may he sit down satisfied with Him
and at rest in Him!

Now, my beloved, has God made over Himself in
His covenant to His people as their rest, so that in
Him they might find rest; and should they not be at
rest in Him? Oh, dear friends, is not God enough
for us? Has He laid Himself under bonds to us, to be
a God to us, and to do as a God for us? And should
we not rest in Him and satisfy ourselves with Him

alone? Surely we should!

2. The second obligation the saints are under to live in God is this: as God has freely made over Himself in His covenant to them, so they have solemnly vouched and chosen Him, and often vouch and choose Him to be their rest and happiness. When the saints first enter into covenant with God, they solemnly choose and vouch Him to be their God and portion, their rest and happiness. Their language to God is: "Lord, my rest, my portion, my happiness, my all forever; I will have none in heaven, or on earth, but Thyself." Thus David had chosen God, and he puts his soul in mind of it: "O, my soul, thou hast said unto God, 'Thou art my Lord' " (Psalm 16:2). He says to his soul, "You have chosen God for your God, your portion, your happiness," and upon this account he calls his soul to rest in God, and in Him he rests (verses 5–6). And as at their first entering into covenant with God, so also often afterwards, upon several occasions, they choose and vouch God for their rest, portion, and happiness forever.

They make new choices of God, and lay new claims to Him as theirs in their procedure of walking with Him. Sometimes, upon occasion of outward troubles and afflictions, difficulties and distress, they make a new choice of God and vouch Him afresh for their rest and happiness. So David said, "I trusted in Thee, O Lord; I said, 'Thou art my God' " (Psalm 31:14). Here he makes a new choice of God, and lays a new claim to Him as his. And when or upon what occasion was this? When he was surrounded with outward troubles, as appears in verses

10–13: "My life is spent with grief, and my years with sighing. I was a reproach among all mine enemies. I am forgotten, as a dead man out of mind. I have heard the slander of many; fear was on every side, they devised to take away my life." And, being thus distressed, he flees to God and chooses Him afresh, and lays a fresh claim to Him. So again, "I looked on my right hand, and beheld, but there was no man that would know me; refuge failed me, no man cared for my soul" (Psalm 142:4–5). Well, what then? Why, he runs to God and vouches Him afresh for His. "I cried unto Thee, O Lord; I said, 'Thou art my refuge, and my portion in the land of the living.' "

So the church, in her great troubles and afflictions, does in like manner: "The Lord is my portion" (Lamentations 3:24). Sometimes, upon occasion of some eminent mercy or deliverance wrought by God for them, they make a new choice of God, and vouch Him afresh to be theirs. So those say, "The Lord is my strength and song, and He is become my salvation. He is my God, and I will prepare Him a habitation, my father's God" (Exodus 15:2). He wrought a signal deliverance for them. He had carried them through the Red Sea and delivered them from Pharaoh and the Egyptians, whom He drowned for their sakes, and now they sing a song of praise to God and vouch Him to be their God. They renew covenant with God, and so their choice of Him, as their rest, their portion, and their all forever. This the church does: "This God is our God forever and ever; He will be our guide even unto death" (Psalm 48:14). God had done great things for her, and hereupon she vouches Him afresh for her.

David often does the like. Sometimes, again, upon occasion of some fresh discoveries made of God in His love and beauty to them, or their being taken into some near and intimate communion with Him, then they choose Him afresh and vouch Him to be theirs afresh. The psalmist said, "Whom have I in heaven but Thee? and there is none upon earth that I desire besides Thee; Thou art the strength of my heart, and my portion forever" (Psalm 73:25–26). Here is a new choice of God made by this holy man, and what was the occasion for it? Why, he had been with God in His sanctuary; that is, he had been conversing with God in His Word and ordinances. He had had some new displays and discoveries of His love, beauty, and excellency made to him; and hereupon he chooses God afresh and vouches Him to be his all, both in heaven and upon earth. So, you know, when the spouse had been led into the banqueting house by Christ, and had had the banner of love displayed over her—when she had been seated by Him in His house of wine—then she made a new choice of Christ and vouched Him for hers afresh. "My beloved is mine, and I am his" (Song of Solomon 2:16).

Thus the saints, both at first and also often afterwards, in their walking with God, have chosen and do choose Him to be their God and portion, their rest and happiness. And should they not then rest in Him? Surely this choice of theirs calls aloud, and should be a mighty obligation upon them, to live at rest in God forever.

3. The third obligation the saints are under to live at rest in God is this: God is at rest in them. As

the saints have chosen God for their rest, so God has
chosen them for His rest, and His soul is at rest in
them. "The Lord hath chosen Zion; He hath desired
it for His habitation. 'This is My rest forever; here
will I dwell, for I have desired it' " (Psalm 132:13–14).
Zion here is a type of the church and people of God,
and as such God's soul is at rest in her. "This is My
rest." The saints are, and to eternity will be, a delight
and solace to the soul of God. God is indeed delighted and at rest in His people above all the works
of His hands; hence the church is called "the delight of God" (Isaiah 62:4). Hence also He is said to
"rejoice over them with joy, to rest in His love upon
them, and to joy over them with singing"
(Zephaniah 3:17). God is in some sort more delighted and at rest in His people than in the angels
themselves; and indeed He sees a greater beauty and
glory upon them than upon the angels. He looks
upon the angels as standing in their own beauty,
their own holiness and righteousness only; but He
looks upon His saints as standing in, and clothed
with, the beauty and righteousness of Christ, and
that is much more glorious than the angels. The
beauty and righteousness of the angels is but the
beauty and righteousness of creatures, but the
beauty and righteousness of the saints is that of Him
who is God-man, God as well as man (Romans 1:17),
and on this account God's soul is more at rest in
them. God is chiefly delighted, and at rest in
Himself and the perfections of His own being. Next
to Himself, His soul is delighted and at rest in
Christ as Mediator: "Behold mine Elect, in whom
My soul delighteth," says the Father of Him in Isaiah

42:1. And, next to Christ the Mediator, His soul is at rest in His saints and people in and through Christ. He looks upon them not as they are in themselves, but as they are in Christ; not as apart from Christ, but as made one with Christ, and so shining in His beauty and clothed with His righteousness; as participating in all His amiableness. He looks upon them not so much according to what they are at present, as according to what they are in the counsels of His own love, and what He intends to make them, and so they are all glorious, both within and without. And accordingly He is delighted in them.

Now is God's soul at rest in them? And should not their souls be at rest in Him? Oh, what a mighty obligation is this upon them always to be at rest in God!

4. The fourth obligation the saints are under to live at rest in God is this: they hope to, and assuredly shall, live at rest in and with God forever in heaven. Heaven is a state of rest. So the Apostle represents it: "There remaineth a rest to the people of God" (Hebrews 4:9). It is a state of rest in God and with God, and in this rest the saints hope to live forever. Hence they are said to have this hope: "everyone that hath this hope" (1 John 3:3), that is, the hope of seeing Christ and being made like Him in the other world, the hope of heaven, the eternal rest. Saints, then, are persons who have this hope; hence also heaven, and the rest to come, is called hope, "the hope which is laid up for you" (Colossians 1:5), and also the blessed hope: "looking for the blessed hope" (Titus 2:13). In both these places, heaven and the coming rest is called hope; for hope here (as

Calvin and others observe) is put for the object of hope, or the good hoped for. But why is it called hope? For this, reason, among others: because it is the great object of the saints' hopes. It is what they hope, look, and long for. And as they hope to, so assuredly they shall live at rest in God, and with God forever; it is what remains to them, and they shall, in due time, attain unto it. Hence it is said to be "laid up for them in heaven" (Colossians 1:5), which (as Calvin also observes) notes the certainty of it, and of their enjoying it. It is what they cannot miss.

When the Apostle speaks of a hope laid up in heaven for us, he signifies to us that the saints ought therefore to rest sure and certain of the promise of eternal life, as if they had a treasure already hidden and laid up in a most safe place.

Now, do the saints hope to, and accordingly shall they live at rest in and with God forever? And should they not be at rest in God here? Surely this is a mighty obligation upon them to be always at rest in Him.

Thus you have seen some of those obligations the saints lie under to live at rest in God, which, though but some of them, yet are sufficient to evince the truth of our position, namely that they should always be at rest in Him.

Chapter Four

*The truth asserted, further evidenced from the
excellency of this frame of soul, the worth
and excellency whereof is discovered
in several particulars*

As the saints are under many great and weighty
obligations to be always at rest in God, so to be always at rest in God is a choice and an excellent
frame and posture of soul for the saints to live in. It
is indeed the best and most becoming frame of soul
that can possibly be found in this world, which may
give further evidence of our assertion. Now I shall
show you a little of the worth and excellency of this
frame and posture of soul in a few Scripture propositions about it.

1. To be at rest in God is a very gracious frame
and posture of soul, a frame and posture of soul
which carries much of the life and power of grace
and godliness in it. And oh, what an excellent frame
and posture must this then be! The more of the life
and power of grace and godliness any frame or posture of soul carries in it, the more excellent it is.
Now there is no frame or posture of soul that I know
of which carries more of the life and power of grace
and godliness in it than does this of being at rest in
God. Herein, indeed, does the main, if not the
whole, of the life and power of grace and godliness

consist; for, pray, what is grace and godliness, and
wherein does it consist, but in a holy subjection to,
and acquiescence in, the blessed God? To bow and
submit to God as our Lord, and to choose and acquiesce in God as our happiness, is grace; this is
godliness—both of which I take to be compre-
hended in Psalm 16:2, where David puts his soul in
mind that he had both given up himself to God, and
also chosen Him for his happiness, saying, "O my
soul, thou hast said unto the Lord, 'Thou art my
Lord, my ruler, my happiness.' "

This, my beloved, is grace or godliness. The
more of this there is found in us, the more gracious
we are. And what is this but to be at rest in God, as
we have opened it? A restless and unquiet spirit argues much of the power of sin, and shows that grace
has gotten but little, if any, dominion in the soul.
And therefore it is made both the character and the
judgment of wicked men that they cannot rest. "The
wicked (says the prophet) are like the troubled sea
when it cannot rest, whose waters cast up mire and
dirt; there is no peace to the wicked" (Isaiah 57:
20–21). It is meant of their own inward unquietness
and restlessness of spirit. Calvin hereby understands
this to be perpetual tossings and perturbations of
mind: "This similitude of a sea is an elegant similitude, and most apt to set forth the inquietude of
wicked men; for the sea is troubled in itself, though
it be not driven by winds, nor tossed with storms and
tempests, but its own waves fight one with another,
and break one another. In the like manner, wicked
men are troubled with intestine evil, which is fixed
and rooted in their own minds."

Thus a restless, unquiet spirit argues much of the power of sin in the soul, and shows that grace has gotten but little, if any, dominion there. So, on the other hand, a spirit at rest in God must carry much of the life and power of grace and godliness in it. This, indeed, is a great part of the kingdom of God, for "the kingdom of God consists not in meat and drink, but in righteousness, in peace, and in the joys of the Holy Ghost" (Romans 14:17). "In peace," that is (as a learned man expounds it), in a holy rest and quiet of soul in God.

2. To be at rest in God is a ready frame and posture of soul, a frame and posture of soul which renders a man ready and prepared for every call of God to him; and must not that be an excellent frame? God, my beloved, may call us to what He pleases, to what services He pleases, and to what conditions He pleases. Besides the general duties of Christianity which are incumbent upon all, He may call us to what special work and services He pleases. He may call us to do, and He may call us to suffer. It is a blessed thing to be fitted and prepared for the call of God, and who is more so than he who lives at rest in Him? Alas, to such a one no work, no duty, no service is unseasonable. Such a one is fit to pray and fit to praise; fit to hear and fit to meditate; fit to search his own heart and fit to inquire into the counsels of God. He is fit to do and fit to suffer the will of God.

"My heart is fixed, O God, my heart is fixed" (Psalm 57:7), or, as you have in the margin in some of your Bibles, "My heart is prepared." If you look back to verse 1, you will find David's soul sweetly at rest in God; for "O God, my soul trusteth in Thee; in the shadow of Thy wings will I make my refuge." And being thus at rest in God, his heart is prepared. It is a ready posture for duty and service. Oh, it is the restlessness and discomposure of our hearts that makes us unfit and indisposed for our work and duty. When the Israelites were filled with anguish of spirit, they could not hear Moses (Exodus 6:9); and when Jonah's spirit was off its rest, though he was an eminent prophet of God, he could not pray but very peevishly and unbecomingly (Jonah 4:2–3). A restless spirit is unfit for the ordinary duties of Christianity. But take a soul who is indeed at rest in God, and he is fit not only for the general duties of Christianity—such as prayer, hearing, or the like— but even for whatever work or duty God shall call him out unto, though never so difficult or mean. Such a one may, in his place and station say, as David spoke to God, "Lord, if Thou wilt make me a shepherd to keep sheep, or if Thou wilt make me a king to govern Thy people, behold, mine heart is prepared. I am in a ready posture for the one or the other."

Oh, what a sweet frame is this! God may also call us to what condition He pleases, to a condition of fullness or of want, of prosperity, affliction, and the like. Now whatever condition He calls to, the soul that is at rest in Him is ready for it. Does God call him to sufferings, to take up and bear the cross? He is ready for this call of God, for he can rejoice, yea, glory in the cross (see Romans 5:3). He can sing in a prison, as Paul and Silas did (Acts 16:25). Does God call him to fullness? He knows how to abound. Does

God call him to want? He knows how to be abased, as Paul did in Philippians 4:12. Does God call him to mourning? He is ready for it; for he, and indeed he alone, knows how to weep as if he wept not. Does God call him to rejoicing? He is ready for it; for he and he alone can rejoice as if he rejoiced not (1 Corinthians 7:30), which is the fittest posture and carriage for each condition.

In a word, he is fit to live and fit to die; and, let me tell you, that is a great word, yet a true one. He is fit to die, ready in good measure for another world. It is a great thing to die, and it is a great attainment to be ready to die; and that is the soul that is at rest in God. I scarcely know a more desirable frame and posture to die in than of being at rest in God. Now if it is a frame of soul which thus renders a man ready for every call of God to him, surely it must then be an excellent frame.

3. To live at rest in God is a safe frame and posture of soul, a frame and posture of soul that secures a man against danger, and therefore an excellent frame. There is not a soul in the world so secure from danger as he who is at rest in God. Such a one is "set aloft." "The name of the Lord is a strong tower the righteous flee thereunto, and are saved" (Proverbs 18:10), or, as the word is, "are set aloft above the reach of danger." They flee to the name, to the nature, to the attributes of God. They retire there, rest there, and are secured against danger. This is what guards and fences the soul, and that against his grand enemy, the devil.

It is a great and sweet Scripture: "The peace of God, which passeth all understanding, shall keep (shall guard or garrison) your hearts and minds through Christ Jesus" (Philippians 4:7). It shall fence and fortify you against temptations; and, indeed, no soul is so fenced and fortified against temptation as he who lives at rest in God. Those temptations which wound others and lead them captive into sin cannot fasten upon him.

A true rest in God is a kind of lifeguard to the soul, and there is no guard like it in the world. It keeps temptation from entering in and it keeps corruption from breaking out. It is a sweet exposition which one gives of Philippians 4:7 ("the peace of God shall keep your hearts and minds"), that is, that rest and tranquility of soul which the faithful have in God shall preserve their hearts as with a military guard and power against the temptations of Satan and the world, and it shall keep their minds stable in Christ.

And to the same purpose also, Calvin said upon that passage, "The peace of God shall keep you. Left by wicked thoughts or desires you would revolt from God." Oh, my beloved, there is scarcely anything that gives the devil and his temptations greater advantage against us than a disturbed, restless, discomposed spirit. Such is evident from Ephesians: "Be ye angry, and sin not; let not the sun go down upon your wrath, neither give place unto the devil" (Ephesians 4:26–27). Here it is clearly intimated that by an unquiet, disturbed spirit we give place unto the devil, and there is scarcely anything on the other hand that so fences and fortifies the soul against Satan and his temptations as a holy rest of soul in God. The saints in heaven are out of all danger, either of sin or temptations. Why so? Truly for this reason, among others: because there they are perfectly at rest in God. They find that perfect solace and satisfaction in God that they cannot possibly admit of sin. Nor have they the least tendency to turn aside to anything else. What shall I say? A soul that is off his rest is off his watch; and, being off his watch, he is in the mouth of danger, whereas it is quite otherwise with a soul at rest in God.

4. To live at rest in God is a very comfortable frame and posture of soul, a frame and posture of soul which is attended with much spiritual comfort and communion with God; which also speaks the excellency of it. A soul living at rest in God usually has the fullest comforts, and the sweetest communion with God, of any on this side of heaven. The truth is, the thing itself carries inexpressible sweetness in it besides God's delight to manifest Himself to those who live in the exercise of it. God (you know) was in the still voice, and there the prophet found Him. He was not in the great and strong wind, He was not in the earthquake, He was not in the fire; but He was in the still voice (1 Kings 19: 11–12). The good prophet had been off his rest in God; he had been in a passion, and under great discomposure of spirit, as you may see in verse 4. And now God gives him this vision of the wind, the earthquake, and the fire to let him see that that was not the way to communion with Him, to caution him against passion and all discomposure of spirit which he was naturally very prone unto.

Oh, God loves to dwell in, and meet with, a sedate, serene, composed spirit, a spirit composed and at rest in Himself; and those who are so are the souls who usually have the clearest sights, the sweetest tastes, the fullest communications of love from Him of all others. They are those who have the most close and constant communion with Him, who are most in His bosom and the embraces of His everlasting arms, who have the most of His Spirit, His presence, His consolations given to them. "Acquaint thyself with God, and be at peace; so shall good come unto thee" (Job 22:21). In other words, in your own spirit, be of a sedate mind; do not rave, do not rage, do not distemper and discompose yourself, as you have done, but be quiet and sedate in your own soul.

Well, but what shall I gain by it? Why, thereby "good shall come unto thee." What good? Not only outward, temporal good, but also spiritual good, the good of grace, the good of divine consolations, the good of communion with God, and the special manifestations of His love. Oh, the more a man's soul is at rest in God, the more full will his comforts, and the more intimate will his communion with God be. As for a restless, disturbed spirit, it is so like the devil (as by and by you will hear) that God cannot come beside it, nor do much in a way of special grace and spiritual comfort for it. Christians complain many times that they have but little communion with God, but little experience of His love and presence with them; and one reason, among others, why they have cause so to complain is that they are not more at rest in God. Were they more at rest in Him, He would rest more in His love, His grace, His presence with and upon them.

5. To live at rest in God is a God-like frame and

posture of the soul which greatly resembles God, is suitable to Him, and brings us up into the very life and blessedness of God Himself; and what a choice frame must it then be! The more likeness and resemblance anything carries in it to God, and the more anything brings us into the life and blessedness of God, the more excellent it is. Now, there is nothing that more resembles God or is more suitable to Him, nothing that brings us more up into the life and likeness of God, than to be thus at rest in Him in our souls. This indeed is the very life and perfection of God, the posture (if I may so speak) which God Himself lives in; for He is ever at rest in Himself. He is infinitely well-pleased with what He Himself does, and rests infinitely satisfied with His own fullness and excellencies.

God is His own rest, His own center. God is infinitely delighted with His own will, infinitely satisfied with His own fullness, and so is at rest in Himself, which indeed is His blessedness. Accordingly, the more our souls are at rest in Him, the more we resemble Him and are brought into His life and His blessedness. A restless, unquiet spirit does, above all things, resemble the devil, and is suitable to the devil. It is, indeed, the very life, image, and spirit of the devil, for the devil is a restless, unquiet spirit, always acting in opposition to God, and always fretting at the dispensations of God. "He seeks rest, but finds none" (Matthew 12:43). As wicked ones cannot rest, so neither can the wicked one rest, but is perpetually disturbed.

Now as a restless, unquiet spirit resembles the devil, and is the very life and image of the devil, so to be at rest in God is what resembles God, and is the very life of God in the soul. It is what brings us up into the divine life, the divine blessedness; and oh, what an excellent frame must this be!

6. To live at rest in God is a God-honoring frame and posture of soul, a frame of soul that does much honor to God and gives glory to Him. Therefore it must have much worth and excellency in it. Of all frames, as well as actions, none honors and glorifies God more than this of being at rest in Him. This gives to God the glory of His sovereignty and the glory of His sufficiency, two of the brightest jewels in the crown of heaven. It owns and acknowledges God to be both best and greatest, the highest Lord and the chief good, and so it glorifies God as God. It sets Him up as God in the soul and gives Him the honor due unto His name as such. Restless, disturbed, unquiet spirits darken and obscure the glory of God. They censure the divine (as one of the ancients speaks of them); they censure the blessedness of God, and, in effect, deny and disown the sovereignty of God, the wisdom of God, the goodness of God, the faithfulness of God, the fullness, sufficiency, and perfection of the Holy One. In effect they say that God's will is not a good, wise, and holy will, that there is not enough in God to satisfy souls and make them happy. Oh, what an affront and dishonor is this to the majesty of heaven!

But, now, the soul that is indeed at rest in God gives Him the glory of all. He sets the crown where it ought to be, and, oh, how much this speaks out the worth and excellency of this frame of soul!

7. To live at rest in God is an honored and highly

esteemed frame and posture of soul, and that by God Himself; a frame and posture of soul which God greatly honors, and puts a great value upon; which also speaks the excellency of it. There is scarcely any frame of soul that God more values, honors and delights in than this of a holy rest in Himself. This is in the sight of God of great price. "Put on the ornament of a meek and quiet spirit, which in the sight of God is of great price" (1 Peter 3:4). In the sight of men, at least unholy and unspiritual men, it is of little price, of no price—they despise and condemn it—but God has other thoughts and other values of it. He highly esteems and honors it. He looks on it as one of the choicest ornaments, as one of the highest excellencies of any soul.

Now, certainly, that is best which God values and honors most. As it is that which honors God most, so it is that which God most honors, and must have the most true worth and excellency in it. A restless, unquiet spirit on the one hand, or a spirit at rest in the creature on the other hand, is what God abhors and despises; but a spirit at rest in Himself He highly values.

8. To live at rest in God is a heavenly frame and posture of soul, a frame and posture of soul which carries much of heaven in it; it is indeed in a great measure the life of heaven here on earth. And what, then, is more excellent than this? Pray, my beloved, what is heaven, and the life of heaven, the life which the saints and angels live in heaven? Heaven is a state of rest (Hebrews 4:9). And what is that rest? True, there is an external rest, a rest from labor and trouble, from conflict and temptation; but the main

feature of it is the inward rest of the soul, that rest and complacency which the soul enjoys in God, and shall enjoy in Him and with Him forever. There the soul is filled with God; he is perfectly swallowed up in the divine will, being thoroughly conformed thereunto, and he has the perfect vision and fruition of the divine glory and fullness, seeing Him as He is (1 John 3:2). And in both of these he is filled with even an infinite contentment and satisfaction of heart. This is the true rest of heaven.

What is the life which saints and angels live? It is a life of perfect rest and solace in God, such rest and solace in God as that they never think of going out to anything else. "God is all in all to them" (1 Corinthians 15:28). Thus to be at rest in God is a heavenly frame and posture of his soul; and, oh, what an excellent frame must this be!

Well, then, lay all these eight things together and you shall find an incomparable worth and excellency in it, which is a further evidence of the saints' duty and interest to live therein.

Chapter Five

---

*The truth particularly improved. The saints called
upon to live thus at rest in God. Arguments
urged to induce them so to do*

What it is for the soul to be at rest in God, what
obligations the saints are under to live at rest in
Him, and the excellency of this frame and posture of
spirit, you have had laid open before you. Now what
shall we say to these things? Oh, that all who profess
themselves to be saints, or would be accounted so,
would give all diligence always to live thus at rest in
God. Possibly some of us are quite off our center; our
souls are full of storms and tempests, tossings and
tumblings; they are not only cast down, but also "disquieted within us" (as holy David's was in Psalm
42:11). Others of us, perhaps, are at rest, but it is a
sinful rest, at rest in the creature and not in God; at
rest in carnal, sensible things. We are of those who
are at ease in Zion; yes, perhaps we are even singing
that requiem to our souls that the fool sometimes
did: "Soul, take thine ease, eat, drink, and be merry;
thou hast goods laid up for thee for many years"
(Luke 12:19).

But now this truth, and the things declared
about it, call upon the one and the other of us to return to God as our rest, and to center purely and entirely in Him alone. This truth calls off the one from

all those unquiet motions and agitations that are within us, from all our tossings and tumblings, to a holy calm and quiet of heart in God; and it calls off the other from all our false rests and reposes to a holy rest and repose in God. And, oh, that both the one and the other would hear and obey this call, taking up our rest in God alone. Oh, my beloved! Are you under such obligations to live at rest in God as you are? And yet will you not live at rest in Him?

On the other hand, is the frame and posture of soul so excellent, and will you neglect it and not study to be found always therein? Let me recapitulate a little particularly. Has God freely made over Himself in all His fullness and riches in His covenant to you as your rest and portion forever, and yet will you not live at rest in Him? Have you chosen God, and vouched Him for your God and portion, and yet will you not live at rest in Him? Is God so much at rest in you, and yet will you not live at rest in Him? Shall you, and do you, hope to live at rest in God and with God forever in heaven, and yet will you not live at rest in Him here? Oh, I think these things should constrain you!

On the other hand, should not the excellency of the frame allure you? Would you live forth much of the life and power of grace? Then live at rest in God. Would you be ready for every call of God to you, whatever to do or to suffer, to live or to die? Then live at rest in God. Would you be fenced and fortified against temptation? Then live at rest in God. Would you enjoy much spiritual comfort and communion with God? Then live at rest in God. Would you be like God? Would you resemble God and grow up

into His life and blessedness? Then live at rest in God. Would you honor God? You have greatly dishonored Him; would you now honor Him? Then live at rest in Him. Would you live in heaven, and begin the life of heaven here on earth? Then live at rest in God.

Oh, why should we think of any other rest but God? Or why should we live in any other posture of soul but this, of a rest in Him? Is there any so sweet, so amiable, so becoming as this? Oh, let us labor, as near as possible, always to be found in this posture. Blessed be God that we may rest in Him.

Two things we should bless God for: One is that there is a rest remaining for us in the other world; whether we find rest here or not, yet there is a rest to come, a blessed rest (Hebrews 4:9). The other is that there is a rest in God for us, and that we may enter into and live in that rest even here. When there is no rest to be had in this world's enjoyments, no rest in or from the creature, yet there is a rest to be had in God and from God. "We that have believed do enter into rest" (Hebrews 4:3). There is a rest in God, in the will, the presence, the love, the fullness of God, which we do or may enter into even here in this world. Blessed be God for this rest, and this is the rest which I am now calling you into.

And yet a little further to set home the call upon you, consider a few things:

1. Consider what a sad and dismal thing it is for a soul to rest in anything but God alone. A rest of one kind or another the soul will have. If God is not its rest, it will take up a rest elsewhere. Now, it is a sad and woeful thing for a soul to rest anywhere but in

God alone. "Woe to them that are at ease in Zion" (Amos 6:1), that is to say, who are at rest in carnal, sensual things in Zion. So the prophet afterwards explains himself (verses 4–6): "woe to them who seek rest in the creatures, who take up their solace and satisfaction in carnal contentments, and not in God." To take up our rest in the creatures and not in God is for us to prefer the creature before God, and to be content with the creature without God, for our portion and happiness forever. And, what is more, it is a dreadful argument that a man's allies are in the creature, and that God intends for him nothing but the creatures forever. "Woe unto you that are rich (says Christ), for you have received your consolation" (Luke 6:24).

"Woe unto you that are rich," that is, "you who rest in your riches (as Calvin rightly expounds it), who take up your happiness in these things." "Woe unto you," and what woe to them? Truly a most dreadful woe: "you have received your consolation (says Christ). You have all the good you are ever likely to have; you shall have no more, and no other happiness or consolation forever. Your resting in these things argues these things to be your all." And, oh, what a woeful, dreadful thing is it for a man to have his all in this world, in a few, vain, empty, bittersweet, perishing vanities here! It was a cutting, killing word which Abraham delivered to Dives when he said, "Son, remember, that thou in thy lifetime receivedst thy good things" (Luke 16:25). He had all his happiness in this world, which is the woe and misery of such as take up their rest anywhere but in God alone. Tremble, then, at this.

2. Consider how impossible it is to find any true rest, solace, and satisfaction of soul anywhere but in God and with God alone. You may as soon find life in death or light in darkness as rest for your souls anywhere but in God alone. Pray, friends, where will you look, or whither will you go to find rest on this side of God and Christ? Will you have recourse to sin, to your lusts? To these, multitudes run; they pursue their rest, solace, and satisfaction from sin, and the pleasures of sin. Yes, as Solomon says, "They rest not, unless they sin," unless they do evil. But, my beloved, is there rest to be found in sin? Can that give rest that is the greatest evil in the world? Can that give rest that is the cause of all our troubles and difficulties? Can that give rest that is the cause of all the confusions and desolations that are in the world? Can that give rest that was the first and only cause and founder of hell? Had there been no sin, there would have been no hell. Can that give rest that makes us like the devil, that restless spirit, yes, and that made him of a glorious angel a devil? Can that give rest that is infinitely contrary to God, that is the only object of His hatred, and that alone can and does separate between God, the chief good, and our souls?

Oh, the folly of souls to pursue a rest in sin, in the satisfaction of a lust! True, a base, brutish pleasure and delight wicked men take in sin, but will it not be bitterness in the latter end? "The wages of sin is death" (Romans 6:23). Yes, and not only death at last, but many times anguish and torment here. Will you have recourse to the good things of this world, to creature comforts and enjoyments, to friends, relations, estate, and the like? In these things thousands make their rest in practice, saying with that rich fool, "Soul, take thine ease, thou hast goods laid up for thee for many years" (Luke 12:19). "You have a good trade, a fair estate, pleasant enjoyments; take your ease, soul, sit down and rest."

But, my beloved, can these things give rest? Alas, it is the joint message of all the creatures to us: "Rest and happiness for your souls is not to be found in us; seek it elsewhere, if you intend to find it."

"The creatures (says a worthy divine) are not good; at least, they are not the soul's good. Nothing but an infinite Godhead can allay your hunger after happiness." Can wind, can vanity, can a shadow, can a fancy, can things of naught, things that are not, things that are even made up of emptiness and changeableness, give rest? Such (you know) these things are in Scripture represented to be. If these things could have given rest, why had not Solomon found it in them? He had certainly the fullest enjoyment of them that ever man had, and, not only so, but moreover he had wisdom and skill to extract the sweetness of them, to improve whatever they have in them, yes, and he improved his wisdom and skill to the uttermost; for he set himself (as he tells us) to enjoy whatever the creature could possibly afford. He gave himself up to a full enjoyment of all.

Well, did he find rest in them after all? No, he was so far from finding rest that he cried out, "All is vanity and vexation of spirit," and this he does often. "All is vanity and vexation of spirit," and can vanity and vexation of spirit give rest? What if a man has an affluence, an abundance of these things, and they are also increasing daily? Will they not afford a rest for him then? No, "He that loveth silver shall not be satisfied with silver, nor he that loveth abundance with increase; this also is vanity" (Ecclesiastes 5:10). Silver, abundance, increase, all is vanity, and cannot give rest.

And, my beloved, does not our experience tell us the same thing? Alas, did we ever find any true rest and satisfaction of soul in these things? True, we are apt to promise ourselves rest in this and that, in this condition and that enjoyment; but did we ever find that which we promised ourselves? Have we not always met with disappointments? We have dreamed of a rest in these things; but it has been but a dream. It has been with us as it is in the prophet: "It shall be as when a hungry man dreameth, and behold he eateth. But he awaketh, and his soul is empty; or as when a thirsty man dreameth, and behold he drinketh, but he awaketh, and behold he is faint, and his soul hath appetite" (Isaiah 29:8). Just so it is, and it has been with us, while we are or have been pursuing rest, and promising ourselves rest in and from the creature.

Yes, and other saints have experienced and asserted the same thing: "All things (said Augustine) are full of trouble and difficulty. Thou alone, O God, are the true rest." And it is a great speech of his, worthy to be written upon the table of all our hearts, speaking to souls who are gone off from God: "Return, you prevaricators, to yourselves, and cleave unto Him that made you. Stand with Him, and you shall stand. Rest in Him, and you shall rest." And again, he says, "Rest and happiness are not to be found where you seek them; seek what you seek, but know that it is not to be found where you seek it. You seek a blessed life in the region of death, and it is not there; for how should a blessed life be found where there is not so much as life itself?"

The sum of all seems to be that those who desert God go from the true rest and happiness of souls; and to seek rest and happiness anywhere but in God and Christ is to seek the living among the dead. Once more, will you have recourse to yourselves and be your own rest? Indeed, we read that "a good man shall be satisfied from himself" (Proverbs 14:14), but how from himself? From himself in union and communion with his God; from himself as in communion with Him who is the chief good, who has all good in Him, and not otherwise. And therefore observe that "the good man" here stands in opposition to the backslider, one who has gone off from God.

Our selves, considered abstractly in themselves, are most insufficient to give rest to the soul, being most vain, changeable, and deceitful. "Every man in his best state is altogether vanity" (Psalm 39:5). It is a great saying I have read in Bernard: "I have sought rest in all things that are seen, but I could not find rest in them; then returning to myself, I found I could not possibly subsist in myself, because my mind is most light and vain." In nothing without, in nothing within, could he find any rest but in God alone.

I will close this argument with a weighty speech which I have read in a worthy divine of our own, blessed Mr. [Jeremiah] Burroughs, who, speaking of

God's being the rest and portion of His people, speaks thus: "Suppose that God should cause all the kings and emperors in the world to come and cast down their crowns at the foot of a holy soul and say, 'All these are thine.' He would answer, 'This is not enough, for this is not God Himself.' Suppose God should bring all the splendors of all the creatures in heaven and earth, and they should be cast at the foot of a holy soul as his; he would say, 'This is not enough, this is not God Himself.' Suppose God should cause all the glory of heaven, not only of sun, moon, and stars, but also of the highest heaven abstract from God, to be laid before a holy soul as his, and he would say, 'This is not enough, this is not God Himself.' Once more, should all the angels come and say to a holy soul, 'We are sent to put all our glory upon you,' he would say, 'This is not enough, for this is not God Himself.' Oh, nothing but God in Christ can give rest to souls."

3. Consider what a blessed rest God is for souls, or that souls may find in God. As there is an utter impossibility of finding rest anywhere but in God, so in Him there is a blessed rest to be found for souls, a full, a perfect, an eternal rest. Oh, my beloved, what can your souls desire, or what are they capable of, that is not to be found in God? Would you have good? It must be good that can give rest to the soul. God is good. He is the chief good, the best, the highest good. He is goodness itself. He is good in Himself, and He is the spring and fountain of all that good that is in the creature. He is so good that He is the good of all good, and nothing has anything of goodness in it but as it resembles Him and

participates of Him. "There is none good but One, that is, God" (Matthew 19:17). "He is good that made me (said Augustine), and He is my good, and in Him do I exult and rejoice before all my other good things whatsoever, and in all my other good things." Would you have a full good? Such a good is God; there is a fullness of all good in Him. "He that overcometh shall inherit all things." How so? "I will be his God" (Revelation 21:7). That is, "I will be his, and in having Me, he will have all in Me." Whatever good, beauty, or excellency there is in the creature, yes, in all the creatures put together, it is all but a small drop or ray to that good, beauty, and excellency that are in God. It is but a small spark to the ocean of the divine goodness. "Lord (said Augustine), all those things which Thou hast made are beautiful, but Thou Thyself art infinitely more beautiful."

God has all kinds and all degrees of good in Him. He is light, life and love, peace and joy, holiness and salvation—everything that is good is or that conduces to the happiness of eternal souls. "Thou, Lord, are that good where no good is wanting (said Augustine), and Thou art always at rest because Thou art Thine own rest."

That little good that is found in the creature is narrow, scanty, and but here and there a drop. But God has all good in a blessed union and conjunction in Him. Oh, how glorious a rest may the soul find in Him! Would you have a suitable and convenient good? Such a good is God. He is a suitable and convenient good, a good suitable to the nature, life, and wants of the soul. Among all your creature enjoyments and contentments, there is nothing suitable either to the nature or life of the soul. They are carnal, sensible things, and so are suitable to the flesh and sensual part, and are pleasing to it; but they have nothing suitable in them to an immortal spirit, nothing that an eternal soul can feed upon. The body may as soon feed upon air and ashes as the soul upon creatures.

But now in God there is that good that is in every way suitable to the soul, to the nature, life, and wants of the soul. The soul is of a spiritual nature, and God is a spiritual good. "God is a spirit" (John 4:24). The soul is of a vast capacity; it is next to infiniteness in its capacity and desires; and God is a vast and comprehensive good, having (as has been shown) all good in Him. Without suitableness in the object to the faculty, there can be no rest. Would you have an original, independent good? Such a good is God. Waters taste most pleasant at the fountainhead. In God you have all good, all sweet, all comfort at the fountainhead. Hence He is said to be a "fountain of living waters," and the creatures "broken cisterns" (Jeremiah 2:13). The fountain has all in and from itself, but cisterns, you know, have no more than is put into them. All the good that is in God, He has it in and from Himself; but the creatures, yes, the best of creatures, angels themselves not excepted, have no more than He puts into them.

Now how much is the fountain to be preferred before a cistern! Would you have a pure and an unmixed good, gold that has no dross, wine that has no water in it? Such a good is God. "God is light, and in Him there is no darkness at all" (1 John 1:5).

All things on this side of God have their mixtures;
they have a dark as well as a bright side. All this wine
is mixed with wormwood, this gold with dross. Who
of us ever met with the creature enjoyment that had
not many impurities? The sweetest rose has its
prickles, and the rarest beauty its spot among the
creatures; but God is in every way a pure and an unmixed good. He is all light, life, love, holiness, and
the like.

Would you have a sweet and satisfying good?
Such a good is God; yes, indeed, there is infinite
sweetness and satisfaction to be found in Him. He
can infinitely delight, ravish, solace, and satisfy the
soul forever. Oh, how sweet, how satisfying are the
sights of God, the tastes and descents of His love!
What a heaven does one sight of God, one descent
of His love, make in the soul! David, casting his eye
upon God as his in covenant, is even ravished with it
and cries out, "The lines are fallen to me in pleasant
places; I have a goodly heritage" (Psalm 16:6). And
elsewhere we read of pleasures, of rivers of pleasures,
of satisfaction, of abundance of satisfaction, and all
as that which souls do or may find in God and in
communion with God (Psalm 36:8). David over and
over tells of sweetness and satisfaction, and satisfaction as with marrow and fatness in but the very
thoughts and meditation of God (Psalm 63:5–6).
Augustine, speaking of God and to Him, often
breaks out into such language as this: "Oh, my God,
my life, my sweetness!"

O sirs! Holy souls who live in communion with
God will tell you that there is no sweetness like that
in God, no love like His love, no comforts like His

comforts. They will tell you that one sight of God, one sensible token of His presence in the soul, has more solace and sweetness in it than all the delights of this world, yes, than many worlds; and they accordingly choose and desire it. Oh, how sweet is it to be led into the banqueting house by Christ, and there have the banner of His love displayed over us, and flagons of that wine poured out into us! How sweet is it to have one sight of the King in His beauty; how much more to walk and converse with Him in His galleries! How sweet is it with God in His sanctuary to have Him reveal Himself, His love, His beauty, His glory to us! "O taste and see how good the Lord is" (Psalm 34:8)!

Would you have a sure, eternal, and unchangeable good, a good that never fades, fails, nor has any period? Such a good is God, and God alone. "From everlasting to everlasting He is God" (Psalm 90:2). But this has been sufficiently spoken to elsewhere.

Well, you see what a blessed rest God is for souls. Why, then, should we ever think of looking anywhere else for rest? Oh, wretched hearts of ours, that will leave this God and go out to a vain world and dying creatures for rest and happiness! In a word, if God has all that in Him which you need or are capable of to give you rest and happiness, then retire solely to Him for it. Now what do you want? Or what are you capable of to give you rest and happiness? Do you want and desire life? "With God is the fountain of life" (Psalm 36:9). Do you want peace? God is "the God of peace" (Romans 16:20), and frequently elsewhere is He so called. Do you want pardon? He is the God of pardons, so the words are in the psalms when He is said to be ready to forgive. And, you know, He has promised to pardon iniquity, transgression, and sin, sins of all sorts and sizes, all degrees and aggravations, if souls come to Him (Hebrews 8:12). Do you want grace? He is "the God of all grace" (1 Peter 5:10). Do you want comfort? He is "the God of all consolation." Do you want mercy? He is the "Father of mercies" (2 Corinthians 1:3). Do you want strength, strength to do, to suffer, to live, and to die? He is "the Lord Jehovah, with whom is everlasting strength" (Isaiah 26:4). Do you want joy? "In His presence is fullness of joy" (Psalm 16:11). Do you want salvation, salvation temporal, salvation eternal? He is "the God of salvation" (Psalm 68:20), and as such the church glories in Him. There is no rest like that which is found in God. Souls need not look elsewhere for rest and happiness, for there is all in God alone.

4. Consider what a restless world you live in, and what a troublesome time you are fallen upon. The more restless this world is, and the more troublesome the times are which we are fallen upon, the more we are concerned to take up our rest in God. Certainly, the world was scarcely ever more restless, nor the times more troublesome, than now. In Zechariah 1:11 we read of a time when the whole world was at rest, excepting only the church of God; but it is even quite contrary now, for now the whole world—church and all—are in a restless, troublesome state. We see and hear of little but wars and rumors of wars, and, as it was of old, destruction upon destruction is cried; and what and when the end of these things will be, who can tell?

In Jeremiah 16:5 we read that God had taken away His peace from that people: " 'I have taken away My peace from this people,' saith the Lord." And truly now He seems to have taken away His peace from the world.

I will leave only two Scriptures with you, one out of the Old and the other out of the New Testament, both of which I am apt to think may have a great application to the present days, and may in a great measure receive their accomplishment in them. The first is Zephaniah 3:8: " 'Wait ye upon Me,' saith the Lord, 'Until the day that I arise up to the prey; for My determination is to gather the nations, that I may assemble the kingdoms to pour out upon them Mine indignation, even all My fierce anger; for all the earth shall be devoured with the fire of My jealousy.' "

The other is Luke 21:25–26: "There shall be signs in the sun, and in the moon, and in the stars (and these we have had), and upon the earth distress of nations, with perplexity, the sea and the waves roaring; men's hearts failing them for fear, and for looking after those things which are coming on the earth; for the powers of heaven shall be shaken." I say nothing, only that I fear that, as we have seen some of these things accomplished, so there will be a more full accomplishment of them, and that when the present generation passes away. Doubtless great storms are coming, and happy they are who have an ark to hide themselves in. God has now great works to do. He has the kingdom of antichrist utterly to destroy, the kingdom of His Son Christ to set up in its luster and glory, the final redemption of His

people to work out, His ancient ones to call in, and
His suffering name, attributes, and glory fully to
right and vindicate. And these things are not likely
to be brought about without great storms, convulsions, and concussions in the world.

Well, and what is the language of all this to us?
Verily this: "Souls, retire into God; take up your rest
in Him; make Him your all, both here and in eternity." And, oh, that we would do so! Then should we
rest in the day of trouble. When Noah foresaw the
deluge coming, "he prepared him an ark to the saving of both himself and family" (Hebrews 11:7).
Surely he is blind, indeed, who does not see a deluge
coming upon the world, a deluge of outward troubles and calamities. Oh, why do we not build an ark
in God by making Him our rest? This God invites
His people into. "Come, My people, enter thou into
thy chambers, and shut thy doors about thee; hide
thyself, as it were, for a little moment, until the indignation be overpast. For, behold, the Lord cometh
out of His place to punish the inhabitants of the
earth for their iniquity" (Isaiah 26:20–21). What is it
for God's people to enter into their chambers and
hide themselves but to retire more into Him, to live
at rest and in communion with Him, to put themselves under His protection, and the like? It is for
them to retire from the world and worldly concerns,
and to make Him all, living and resting wholly in
Him and upon Him. Oh, let this, the restlessness of
the world you live in, draw your souls into a holy rest
with God.

5. Consider what enemies you are to your own
souls by not living at rest in God. "He that sinneth

against Me wrongeth his own soul" (Proverbs 8:36). He who lives not at rest in God greatly sins, and thereby greatly wrongs his own soul. On the one hand, you hereby deprive your souls of much good; on the other hand, you expose your souls to much evil.

(1) Hereby you deprive your souls of much good, yes, of much of the best good. Solomon found this in experience, and tells us that by pursuing rest and happiness in the creature, and not in God, he thereby bereaved his soul of good (Ecclesiastes 4:8). What good? Verily, the best good, the good of grace, of holiness, of communion with God, of the comforts of His Spirit, and the like. And, oh, how much of this good do you bereave your souls of daily? This is that which has bereaved you of much grace, much love, much spiritual comfort, many embraces in the arms and bosoms of Christ's love. This (namely, our pursuing rest from the creature and not living at rest in God) is that which has made us so lean, so dead, so dry, so barren in our spirits, as we are. Oh, my beloved, while we have been off our rest in God and have taken up in other things, what have we been doing but feeding upon husks and dregs when we might have eaten bread and drunk wine in the Father's kingdom? What have we been doing but following after lying vanities to the forsaking of our own mercies? Oh, if you knew how sweet a life it is to be at rest in God, you would then know what good you have bereaved your souls of by not living at rest in Him.

(2) Hereby you expose your souls to much evil. I remember a saying of Augustine: "In this I sinned,

that I sought my happiness not in God, but in His creatures, and so I rushed upon all manner of sorrows, confusions, and errors of soul." And have not we done so? Oh, the wounds, the confusions, the errors of soul which we have exposed ourselves unto while we have been off our rest in God! Sin and Satan have made great waste and desolation upon our spirits, and it is what exposes us to nothing but sorrows, snares, and death. And as we would not wrong our souls, let us retire to and live at rest in God.

6. Consider that your living at rest in God here will be a clear and unquestionable evidence to you that you shall live at rest in God and with God forever. Oh, how sweet is it to have any one clear evidence of living at rest in God and with God in heaven! And what would some of our souls give for such a blessing! Yes, how sweet is a small glimpse of hope, a secret whisper, an inward hint or intimation of such a thing from the Spirit of God in our souls? Oh, live at rest in God here, and this will be a broad evidence of it to you. And, truly, unless you live at rest in Him here, I know not, however you will make it out to your souls, that you shall live at rest in Him and with Him in the other world.

In short, my beloved, if we indeed desire to live at rest with God forever in heaven, why should we not desire to live at rest in God here? Sure I am, the thing is the same; and we should desire the one as well as the other, and the one as the evidence of the other. Oh, come, come, and be prevailed with by these things, one and all, to take up the rest of your souls purely and solely in God!

Chapter Six

*Several plain and proper directions to souls how
to attain in this life a rest in God, with a
conclusion of the whole matter*

To live at rest in God is a sweet, blessed life indeed; but how may we attain to it? Our souls would
be at it, but how may we come up hereunto? Let me
give a few directions in that case, and I will close all.

1. Would you indeed live at rest in God? Then despair of ever finding rest anywhere but in Him
alone. As long as we have any hopes of a rest anywhere else, we will not so purely take up our rest in
God as we should; for woe and alas for us, our "heart
is bent to backsliding from Him" (Hosea 11:7). We
are carnal and sensual, and are addicted to carnal
and sensual things. As ever therefore you would live
at rest in God, utterly despair in yourselves of ever
finding rest, yes, anything of rest anywhere else. The
more we are driven out of the creature, out of all our
false rests and reposes, the nearer we are to a holy
rest and repose in God. It has been sufficiently evidenced and declared that there is no true rest for a
soul but in God alone, and you have seen and heard
it; but, my beloved, it is one thing to hear this with
the ear and another thing for the soul to come under sense and power thereof so as, indeed, to be
dead in our hopes to all other things, and practi-

cally to despair of rest and happiness anywhere but
in God alone. Whatever we pretend or profess, at
least most of us, we still think that there is some
rest, some happiness, in something else besides God
and short of God, else what do our eager desires after other things, our delights in them when enjoyed,
our grief and sorrow of heart when they are lost or
wanting mean? What does the secret bend and bias
of our heart to stand off from God and cleave to
other things mean? But all this must be rooted out,
firming and fixing this foundational principle in
your souls, that there is no rest for a soul but in God
alone; and, accordingly, never have a thought of
looking elsewhere. And when at any time the heart
would be going out to other things, check it with
this consideration of rest; for the soul is to be found
only in God.

2. Would you indeed live at rest in God? Then labor to know Him much, and to know Him in Christ.
The more we know God, the more we shall love
Him; and the more we know and love Him, the more
shall we rest in Him. "They that know Thy name
(said the psalmist) will trust in Thee" (Psalm 9:10);
they will rest in God and depend on God. One great
reason why we do not rest in God is that we do not
know Him, at least so know Him as to carry in us
right notions and apprehensions of Him. Labor,
therefore, to know God more and better; labor to
know Him in Christ. God in Christ is most sweet,
most lovely, most ravishing and solacing to souls.
God in Christ is a God of love, yes, a God that is love.
"God is love" (1 John 4:8). God in Christ is a God of
reconciliation: "God was in Christ reconciling the

world unto Himself, not imputing their trespasses to them" (2 Corinthians 5:19); and, oh, how sweet is God thus known! God in Christ is "the Father of mercies, the God of all comfort" (2 Corinthians 1:3). He is a full, free, open fountain of all spiritual good. We read of "the light of the knowledge of the glory of God shining forth in the face of Christ" (2 Corinthians 4:6). And, indeed, the light and glory of God, His beauty, sweetness, and excellency, shines forth nowhere so brightly and illustriously as in Jesus Christ. To know God or to look on Him outside of Christ is what rather fills the soul with trouble than brings it to rest in Him. "I remembered God, and was troubled" (Psalm 77:3). God out of Christ is no other than an angry judge, a consuming fire, one who is ready to damn and destroy the soul; but in Christ He is a God of pardon, a God of salvation to all who come by Christ to Him. Hence some of the saints have profited that they dare not think of God out of Christ. And you know what Luther's thoughts were by that outcry of his, "I will have nothing to do with an absolute God." Oh, therefore labor to know God in Christ more; being known in Him, He is infinitely sweet to souls, and they cannot but find that sweetness in Him that shall draw and allure them to make Him their rest and all forever.

3. Would you indeed live at rest in God? Then labor to get your covenant interest in, and relation to, God cleared up to you. The clearer your interest in God is to you, the fuller and more constant will your rest in Him be. And, indeed, you will never so fully and sweetly acquiesce in God as you should until you come to some good sense of your interest in Him,

and relation to Him in Christ and the covenant. It is said that "David encouraged himself in the Lord his God" (1 Samuel 30:6). He saw God to be his God, and seeing Him to be so he encouraged himself in Him; he sat down satisfied and at rest in Him, and that in the midst of many, great, and sore distresses, as you may there see. Had he not seen Him to be his, I question whether he would have been able to sit down at rest in Him as he did, especially in so great a storm.

So the church: " 'The Lord is my portion,' saith my soul; 'therefore I will hope in Him' " (Lamentations 3:24). Seeing God to be her portion, she could hope, trust, and rest in Him, and that in a case of great calamity and distress. I will not say a soul cannot rest in God without a sense of his interest in Him; no, it is the soul's duty to rest in God however things go with him. Though he is in the dark, though God has withdrawn Himself from the soul, yet the soul should trust in the name of the Lord, and rest himself in his God (Isaiah 50:10). Still there is that in God that is a full and proper matter or ground of rest in Him, for He is as high, as holy, as wise, as good, as all-sufficient as ever He was; and indeed we should learn to believe in the dark. But though this is so, yet still, I say, the clearer your interest in God is to you the more fully and sweetly will you rest in Him. The sense of an interest in God is most effectual to reduce a soul to its rest in God when through temptation it has been carried off from it. So we find it in Psalm 42:11. As ever, therefore, you would live purely and entirely at rest in God, get your interest in Him as your God and

Father cleared up to you. First choose Him for your God and portion; do it every day; never rest until you can say, "Lord, whom have I in heaven but Thee? and there is none upon earth that I desire besides Thee. My heart and my flesh fail, but God is the strength of my heart, and my portion forever" (Psalm 73:25–26). Then pray hard for the sealings and witness of the Spirit. Beg the Lord, with Augustine, to say unto your soul, "I am thy salvation."

4. Would you indeed live at rest in God? Then meditate and contemplate Him much; dwell much in the view of His glorious excellencies and perfections. Deep and frequent meditation on God and His excellencies marvelously endears God unto souls, and withal brings them into an acquaintance with those satisfying delights that are to be found in Him, and so to rest in Him. "My soul (said David) shall be satisfied as with marrow and fatness, and my mouth shall praise Thee with joyful lips, when I remember Thee upon my bed, and meditate on Thee in the night watches" (Psalm 63:5–6). In verse 3 he is even ravished with the sense and perceptions of God's love to him: "Thy lovingkindness is better than life; my lips shall praise Thee;" and here he speaks of satisfaction, the sweet satisfaction which came in a way of holy meditation. Again, "my meditation of Thee shall be sweet" (Psalm 104:34). Holy meditation on God produces many sweet experiences of God in the soul, experiences of His grace, of His love, of His sweetness, of the blessedness of communion with Him, and the like; and these experiences issue in the soul's rest in Him.

Every new experience of God draws the heart further into God, and makes it center more in Him. Every taste, every sight of God, every new emanation of His glory before the soul (of which, in the holy meditation of God, the saints have not a few) weans and works the heart off from carnal, sensible things, and makes him cleave more closely and entirely to God, gathering in about Him as his all. Oh, be much in the meditation of God. It is not enough for us to know Him, and to know Him in Christ, no, nor to know Him as ours, as our God in covenant; but we must study Him; we must meditate on what a God He is, and single Him out, now under one and then under another notion or consideration; to meditate upon Him, begging God to help us in our meditations on Him. Most people know and enjoy little of God because they meditate upon Him so little in holy meditation.

5. Would you indeed be at rest in God? Then improve all your experiences of the creature's vanity toward the carrying of your souls more into God as your rest and center. Holy David did so, and it is indeed a great piece of a Christian's skill. "And now, Lord, what wait I for? My hope is in Thee" (Psalm 39:7). If you view either the foregoing or following part of the psalm, you will find that David was under great experiences of the creature's vanity. He saw the vanity of worldly enjoyments, and saw that they are all but a vain show. He saw his own vanity; he saw the vanity of others; he found everyone and everything to be nothing but vanity. And what is the result? What use does he make of it? This: he gathers in more to God as his only rest and happiness. "Now, Lord, what wait I for? My hope is in Thee." As

if to say, "Now I have done with creatures. I see what
they are, and what all persons and things are, and I
have done with all. Thou Thyself only, O Lord, are
my rest, my happiness, my all."

Thus, when at any time you meet with fresh experiences of the creature's vanity, apply them to the
carrying of your souls more into God as your rest.
You scarcely live a day wherein you do not meet with
new experiences of the creature's vanity. This is lost
and that is embittered to you; now you meet with
disappointments, and that where, it may be, you expected your chief comfort and satisfaction. Now in
all such cases, what should we do? Retire the more
unto God as our rest and happiness. Say with the
psalmist, "Now, Lord, what wait I for? My hope is in
Thee. I have done with the streams; I will cleave only
to Thee, the fountain. The creatures ever serve me
thus: they leave me under sorrows, snares, and disappointments. Thou, Lord, shall be all in all to me.
Thou art my only rest forever."

6. Would you indeed live at rest in God? Then
pray for much spirituality of heart, much suitedness
of spirit to God and Christ. The more spiritual you
are, the more are you suited to the blessed God; and
the more you are suited to God, the more fully and
genuinely will your souls rest in Him. I suppose you
have a new heart (for I speak unto you as to saints);
the old heart, to be sure, will never rest in God; the
old heart is wholly averse to God, and at enmity with
Him. It hates Him; it is wholly carnal, sensual, and
unclean, and delights only in things suitable to itself. Let all, therefore, who would rest in God, first,
get a new heart, such as God promises in His

covenant (Ezekiel 36:26), and, having gotten a new heart, pray for much spirituality of heart and affection. Alas! Alas! We are carnal (as Paul charged his Corinthians), and being carnal we lean to, and hanker after, carnal things; and until we get more spirituality we shall not rest so fully in God as we should. Therefore pray unto God hard for more of this; pray for more of His Spirit, to act upon and influence you; and, not only so, but to change you more and more into the divine life and image.

To conclude all, live at rest all that ever you can in God here, but withal look for, long for, and hasten to that rest which remains for saints with God in the other world. True rest in God here is sweet, but we shall never be fully and perfectly happy until we enter that future rest. That, indeed, carries a complete happiness in it. Oh, to be wholly swallowed up in the divine will, the divine life, the divine fullness, the ocean of divine love, to have every faculty and every affection perfectly suited to God and filled with God—this cannot but be perfect rest and happiness, especially considering what an enlargement there will be of all the faculties, and how much of God they will then take in. But until we reach this rest we cannot have any complete rest; therefore aspire after the future rest. Keep your eye much there, and let your eye affect your heart; look and love, love and long, long and hasten to that sweet, that holy, that heavenly, that inviolable, that unchangeable and eternal rest which remains for saints in God and with God in the other world, crying out, both in your spirits and lives, "Come, Lord Jesus, come quickly." Amen.